CHRIST SUPREME

ISBN 0-946351-20-1

Copyright 1990 by John Ritchie Ltd.
40 Beansburn, Kilmarnock, Scotland

Printed by Bell and Bain Ltd., Glasgow

CHRIST SUPREME

AN EXPOSITION OF THE
EPISTLE TO THE HEBREWS

BY

J. CHARLETON STEEN

OF LONDON

JOHN RITCHIE LTD.
PUBLISHER OF CHRISTIAN LITERATURE
40 BEANSBURN, KILMARNOCK, SCOTLAND KA3 1RH

CONTENTS

PREFACE

AFTER having been saved a few months I had a very dark experience. I was not making headway in the things of God, nor getting an intelligent interest in my bible. I was finding its study becoming increasingly difficult, and altogether I was getting into a bad way. In my despair I went to an elderly brother in Greenock and asked him if he could help me how to read and study my bible with interest and profit. "Yes!" he said, "take the Epistle to the Hebrews, your concordance and a good reference Bible, and begin to study it, sentence by sentence. You will find it will open up to you the great types of Christ's person and work, and give you such an insight into God's ways, that you will become increasingly and intelligently established in the faith, and will find your Bible a perfect joy to your soul." I thanked him, and his advice I began to carry out, rising every morning between five and six for the study of Hebrews. To those early morning studies I owe every thing of what I am, as well as what I have been enabled to do for God ever since. This was in 1883, and from then till now I have lived and revelled in this wonderful letter. I do not mean by this to suggest that I have mastered or exhausted it, for increasingly I feel that I am just touching its fringe; but some of the results of a life's study I, with joy, pass on to fellow believers, praying that it may lead all, but especially young ones, to a study of this, the greatest of all the epistles, and to study it with the same blessed results. It is not an easy study, for it contains " some things hard to be understood." The first and important thing to notice is the address on the envelope. The letter is addressed to " Hebrews." When a letter arrives at our home the first thing we do is to read the envelope to see for whom the letter is. This is one of the last things God's saints do when dealing with His letters. Remember that while *all* God's word is for *all* God's people in *all* time, *all* God's word is not *addressed* to, nor about, *all* God's people in all time.

Miles Coverdale says, " It shall greatly help thee to understand scriptures if thou mark, not only what is spoken or written, *but* of whom, and *to* whom, with *what* words, at *what* time, *where!* to what intent, with what circumstance considering what goeth before and what followeth." This, indeed, is sound advice to which we must give heed if we are to rightly divide the word of truth.

This epistle was sent to Hebrews. I am sure that we who are Gentiles find most of our difficulties in the letter arising from this fact, for we are *not* Hebrews, we have not had their training nor view point. We cannot think Hebrew. Therefore please note it was written to Hebrews. Again, it is quite clear they were Hebrews who had accepted as Saviour and Messiah, " Jesus, the Nazarine." There is abundance of proof of this throughout the epistle. Yet! it was not originally sent to every believing Hebrew wherever found, for those to whom it came were in a backsliding state of soul. They were dull of hearing, "and had become such as had need of milk and not of strong meat" (Heb. v. 12-14). Then, again, they are seen in a defined area and together, for the writer says,

" Timothy is set at liberty with whom, if he come shortly, I will see you " (Chapter xiii. **23**).

The letter stands in our Bibles as anonymous, but, remember that those who first received it knew perfectly well by whom it was written. "I will see you " (Chapter xiii. 23). The association of its writer here with Timothy almost fixes him as Paul.

Very much has been written *re* the authorship of this letter. I am not very much interested in these writings. No matter who the amanuensis was, God Himself is the author of the epistle. Personally, I am satisfied Paul wrote it, and I feel that this is proved *to the very hilt* by 2 Pet. iii. 15-16. Peter wrote to saved Hebrews, and to these he distinctly says, " Our beloved Paul wrote . . . as also in all his epistles." Now this is the only letter addressed to the Hebrews as such, beside those of Peter and James, therefore Paul must be its writer, else there is a Pauline epistle lost, which I would not admit. Hence according to Peter's Epistle, Paul wrote the Hebrews. I also see internal evidences in the letter itself, that stamp it Pauline.

The object of the epistle was to deliver from, and to prevent a return to, Judaism. The delinquent in this letter is " spiritual " and not *moral*. The sin from which to save is " Apostacy." The one argument unto this end used throughout the entire letter is the *superiority* and *supremacy* of Christ in His rank as Son over all that pertained to Judaism.

In Chapters I. and II. Greater than its prophets, and greater than angels. In Chapter III. Greater than Moses. In Chapter IV. Greater than Joshua. In Chapter V. Greater than Aaron. In Chapter VII. Greater than the whole Aaronic priesthood. In Chapter VIII. Greater than the old covenant and its ministers. In Chapters IX. and X. Greater than all its sacrifices and ritual and economy. In Chapter XI. Greater than all its great ones. Its witnesses of faith, for He is seen in Chapter XII. as the author and finisher of faith. In Chapter XIII. He is seen greater than its altar and its great sin-offering, for He was the substance of which they were only shadows. Then comes the command, the final word, " Let us go forth unto Him outside its camp (Judaism) bearing His reproach." It is from these pictures of Him I have derived the title of this volume, " Christ Supreme." May God's gracious Holy Spirit Himself, make real and actual in our hearts the great revelations and visions of Christ presented by Him in this letter, so that we, too, may hear the " Come Forth " of His Lordship outside every camp of Christendom, and go forth to Himself. " The Homeless Stranger." Such is not only my object in writing it, but will be my constant prayer in following it.

For the list of words peculiar to the epistle, and not found elsewhere in the New Testament writings, I am indebted to Bishop Westcott's commentary on the epistle. To those who would like to study it more in detail in connection with the Old Testament's types and shadows, I would recommend that excellent little book by the late Miss Ada Habershon, " *Illumined Hebrews*," published by the Scripture Gift Mission, 14 Bedford Street, Strand, London, W.C. This is a most excellent little work and calculated to help much.—Yours sincerely,

J. CHARLETON STEEN.

ROSENEATH,
   BUCKHURST HILL,
      ESSEX.

CHRIST SUPREME

CHAPTER I

CHRIST—" THE SON OF GOD "

GREATER THAN PROPHETS AND ANGELS

THE opening verses of this Chapter, verses 1-3, for grandeur and greatness stand unsurpassed in all Greek literature. They claim, in no uncertain words, divine authorship for the Old Testament documents. The prophets, men who lived in different times, over one thousand years separating the first from the last, composed of all kinds of men taken from all classes, from the poorest peasant to the king on his throne, educated and illiterate, with differing minds and characters and environments are used by God, as the channels of His revelation, but, only one author, God Himself. " Truly God spake all these words."

> " Whence but from heaven could men unskilled in arts
> In several ages born, in several parts,
> Weave such agreeing truths ? or how, or why,
> Should all conspire to cheat us with a lie ?
> Unasked their pains, ungrateful their advice,
> Starving their gains, and martyrdom their price."
> *Dryden.*

The same God, *Who* in time past spake to the fathers in the prophets, is the one *Who* at the end of these days speaks to us in a Son. This is that which characterises God's speakings to-day, He speaks in a Son, *Who* is the one and only, the perfect, complete, and final revelation of God. This in contrast to the piecemeal and incomplete speakings in the prophets in the past with its many parts, and many ways. God spake in the past by type shadow, similitude, history, allegory, prophecy, etc., here a little and there a little, and in ways that were imperfect as to their mode and result. Now, *He* speaks in one uniform way, and not in parts, but in His full-orbed Christ, the perfect and complete and final revelation of God to man.

"In a Son!" And what a *Son!* He has a past, for by Him He made the ages, He is the Everlasting Father (Isa. ix. 6), *i.e.*, the "Father of the Ages." He is the one who made them, shaped them, upholds and controls them, whatever the ages mean and contain. Whenever they began or finish, the Son is behind every scene, and is also controlling every scene He is behind. The pleasure of the Lord is prospering in His hand. (*See* Isa. liii. 10 ; John iii. 35 ; xiii. 3.)

He has a present, for after making purification for sins He sat down at the right hand of the Majesty on high (verse 3), to fulfil His present session, His mediatorial work.

He has a future, for in verse 6, R.V., we read " And when He again bringeth in the first-born into the world He saith, ' and let all the angels of God worship him.' "

The word for " world " in verse 6 is " The habitable world." This takes us forward to His second advent, to His manifestation in glory, and ours, too, with Him. (*See* Col. iii. 4.)

To me this first chapter is the greatest and fullest chapter in all the Word of God, emphasising in language, the simplicity and grandeur of which cannot be surpassed, the Eternal Godhead of the Eternal Son. Please note it is expressly stated, that it is as Son He is all this. The effulgence of God's glory, the impress of God's substance, creator and upholder of all, eternal, incarnate, enthroned, immutable.

> " Of the full Deity possessed
> Eternally Divine."

His omnipotence, omniscience and omnipresence is glistening throughout the whole. We are not only taken to heights our finite minds can never scale, but also to depths they can never fathom. We see one glory upon another heaped on His devoted Head — the Head of the Everlasting Word; the Father's only Son. Mary's womb never detracted one iota from His eternal attributes. As He lay in the manger, " He *is* Christ the Lord " (Luke iii. 11). The kosmetic activities of the Everlasting Word never ceased.

> " No less Almighty at His birth
> Than on His throne supreme,
> His shoulders held up Heaven and Earth,
> While Mary held up Him."

Do I understand it ? No ! but I do believe it with all my heart !

This wonderful chapter brings Him before us in His glorious future, addressed by God His Father.

" Thy throne, O God, is for ever and ever." Verse 8, assures us that His wounded feet will yet ascend the throne, His thorn crowned brow will yet be covered with many diadems, and His pierced hands will yet sway in sovereignty Earth's sceptre.

> " That Jesus will reign where'er the sun
> Doth his successive journeys run."

In John i. 18 He is spoken of as God's Only-begotten. There He is absolutely alone and unique. No union there, but here in Heb. i. 6 He is brought before us as God's " First-begotten." In this title He is not alone, but is seen associated with men and things and, wherever so found, He is supreme. If we think of Creation, then He is the First-born of all Creation (Col. i. 15). If we think of the dead, He is the First-born from among the dead (Col. i. 18). If we think of man's salvation, we read, " That He might be the First-born among many brethren " (Rom. viii. 29). If we think of earth's kings, then we hear God say, " I will make Him, my First-born, higher than earth's Kings " (Psalm lxxxix. 27). As First-born He is supreme.

ANALYSIS OF CHAPTER I

1. *The Prophet* . " Spoken to us in His Son " (v. 2).
2. *The Priest* . " When He had by Himself purged our sins " (v. 3).
3. *The King* . . " The sceptre of Thy King-dom " (v. 8).

THE PLAN OF THE CHAPTER.

1. *His Rank* . . A Son (v. 2).
2. *His Dominion* . Throne, Sceptre, Kingdom (v. 8).
3. *His Eternal and Creative Powers* (v. 2).
4. *His Imperishability* " Thou remainest " (v. 11).
5. *His Immutability* " Thou art the same " (v. 12).

I.—DISPENSATIONS CONTRASTED.

Past Dispensation. " God spake." How ?
1. Fragmentarily. " In many parts " (v. 1, R.V.).
2. Multifariously. " In many ways " (v. 1, R.V.).
3. Instrumentally. " In prophets " (v. 1).

Present Dispensation. " God spake." How ?
1. Fully and completely. In a Son (v. 2).
2. In one uniform manner—Christ in manhood is the full, complete, and final revelation from God to men.

II.—CHRIST AND PROPHETS CONTRASTED.

Christ's *Sevenfold Superiority* over prophets (vv. 2, 3).
1. A Son.
2. Heir of all things.
3. Creator of the ages.
4. Exact impress of His essence.
5. Effulgence of God's glory.
6. Upholder of all things.
7. Sin-purger.

Confirming the Scriptures (vv. 5, 6).
1. His Sonship (Psalm 2).
2. Heir of David (2 Sam. vii. 14).
3. Coming in glory, and worshipped (Psalm xcvii, 7 ; Deut. xxxii. 43, Septuagint version).

III.—CHRIST AND ANGELS CONTRASTED.

He.
1. The Son (v. 2).
2. Creator (v. 2).
3. Worshipped (v. 6).
4. Author of salvation (Heb. v. 9).
5. Ruler (Heb. ii. 5).

They.
1. Servants (v. 7).
2. Creatures.
3. Worshippers (v. 6).
4. Ministers of salvation (v. 14).
5. Ruled (chap. ii. 5).

IV—CHRIST AND CREATION CONTRASTED.

The Creator—
1. Unchangeable. " Thou art the same (v. 12).
2. Eternal. " Thou remainest " (v. 11).

The Creation—
1. Perishable. " They shall perish " (v. 11).
2. Changeable. " They shall be changed " (v. 12).

Messiah Suffering.
1. His Cry (Psalm cii. 23, 24).
2. God's Answer (Heb. i. 10, 12 ; Psalm cii, 24, 27).

Messiah Reigning (vv. 8, 9).
1. Thy Throne.   " Eternal " (v. 8).
2. Thy Kingdom. " Righteousness " (v. 8).
3. Thy Anointing " Above Thy fellows " (v. 9).

The following words are peculiar to this Chapter and nowhere else found in the New Testament :—

1. **Πολυμερως**—polumerōs, v. 1, translated "sundry times."
   Revisers translate " diverse portions."
2. **Πολυτροπως**—polutropōs, v. 1, translated " diverse manners."
3. ἀπαύγασμα—apaugasma, v. 3, translated " brightness." Revisers translate " effulgence." The R.V. gives the better rendering of this word. It emphasises His Godhead. It reminds us of the creed " Light of Light."

4. **Χαρακτηρ**—character, v. 3, translated " express
image." Revisers' text translate " the very
image," but in their margin they give the
better translation, " the impress." The
thought is the impress of the signet on the
wax. It is the origin of our English word
" character." So our Lord is the impress of
His substance, and that in His manhood. In
Colossians (i. 15) He is called the image of
the invisible God. The word there for image
being (eikōn).

5. **λειπουργικα**—leipourgika, v. 14, translated
" ministering."

Words Nos. 3 and 4 are used in the Apochrypha
and in The Septuagint. No. 5 is found in The
Septuagint.

CHAPTER II

CHRIST—" THE SON OF MAN "

HIS TRUE HUMANITY

IF Chapter I. is occupied with the Deity of the
Lord, this wonderful chapter brings prominently
before us His true humanity. In Chapter I. we
have the fine gold, here we have the Shittim wood,
which foretold His sinless and incorruptible
humanity. If Chapter I. emphasises His power,
as Son of God, to save, this chapter reveals His
right, as Son of Man, to save. In verses 1-4 we
have a solemn exhortation to take heed to the
things which we have heard. The "for" of
verse 2 introduces the argument for the exhortation. Salvation, yea, " so great salvation," is
God's final word, and if we neglect it, how shall
we escape ? The increased privilege carries with
it increased responsibility. The " we " is emphatic, we to whom God speaks in a Son. We
might ask the question here. Escape what ?
The answer is surely in verse 2, " a just recompense
of reward." The word for just here (ενδικον) is
only used once again in this form in Rom. iii. 8,
and the word translated " recompense of reward "
(μιο θαποδοσια) is peculiar to Hebrews, and is
found no where else (see Heb. x. 35 ; xi. 26).
Whatever punishment was meted out to the
covenant people who transgressed and disobeyed
the spoken word, it was a just recompense.
For instance, the man who gathered sticks on the
Sabbath was stoned to death, other minor offences

were dealt with justly, if not so severely, but no transgression escaped ; surely we gather from this passage, that this day of grace does not in any way give us a licence to transgress or disobey God's word, but really increases our responsibility and makes disobedience to-day a much more terrible sin than it was in a past age. We must not limit this word salvation to the initial act of faith which saves. No ! for God's salvation begins with the simple act of faith in Christ which saved, and goes on saving right throughout our pilgrim life, saving from every one, and thing, contrary to the will of God. There is no moment in the believer's life when he can neglect it with impunity.

From verse 5 God continues the subject dealt with in the close of Chapter i., viz., Christ's supremacy over angels. " For unto angels did He not put in subjection the habitable world that is coming," but to man. Then Psalm viii. is introduced to prove this. The reference here to this psalm and its application to Christ makes it Messianic and prophetic. Adam is indoubtedly in it, but a greater than Adam is there, viz., the last Adam, the second man.

In Psalm viii. God gives sovereignty to Adam ; he was God's vicegerent and king, but he became the first rebel and lost all. Not simply for himself but also for his race. This was God's opportunity to introduce the Second Man, the last Adam, and the spirit of God reveals the great truth, that it is the Second Man and not the first, Who is to possess earth's sovereignty.

" But now we see not yet all things subjected to Him," verse 8, *i.e.*, the first man, Adam. Why ? because of sin, he forfeited his right to this sovereignty. The verb for see here is (ὁρῶμεν) differing from the verb to see in verse 9 **(βλεπομεν.)** *i.e.*, to look upon. But we look upon Him . . . even Jesus. Although the first man sinned, fell and failed and forfeited his every right, yet it is written of him. Thou didst " put all things under his feet," verse 8, *i.e.*, Thou didst by one eternal decree. To man God gave it, and man will yet have it, *but* it awaits its fulfilment in the Second Man, the last Adam and His race. Not angels but man.

> " O lovely wisdom of our God
> When all was sin and shame,
> A second Adam to the fight
> And to the rescue came.
> O wisest love that flesh and blood
> Which did in Adam fail
> Should strive afresh against the foe,
> Should strive and should prevail."

The difficulty of the Jew was, how the glorious person of Chapter I. could possibly be the Nazarene, the lonely Stranger who had not where to lay His head, the One who died on a Roman gibbet. The writer in this wonderful chapter sets himself to explain the how of it and the why of it.

Was He lower than the angels ? It was only for a little while, and that for the suffering of death. Did He die ? Yes ! but He died not for Himself, but for others ; He tasted death for every man. Here we have more than the great salvation. We have the great Saviour. In Chapter I. He is greater than angels in rank, dominion, creative and eternal powers. Here He is seen lower than they. Jesus is the one man of whom it could be said " made lower than the angels," the only man to whom this was a humiliation. To every other man it was a glory to be, as Psalm viii. R.V. puts it, " made a little lower than God," but to *this Man* it was a descent, a humilia-

tion. To man "a little lower" was in degree,
but thank God, to Christ it was not a *little of degree*
but a *little of time*, and *that* with a view to death.
But when as first-born He comes again as ruler
into this habitable earth, we read " Let all the
angels of God worship Him " (Chapter i. 6). They
the worshippers, He the worshipped. They the
ruled, He the ruler.

One has well said, " The full thesis is, first lower,
then higher. Nay ! a higher in the lower."

We see Him set forth as a Captain worthy of
God. Isaiah lv. 4 says " I have given Him a
leader and commander to the people." He has
God's sons to bring to glory. He is the Federal
Head of a race, a new creation. He has children
given Him by God. These He has to bring to
glory.

His fitness for that great work lay in a pathway
of sufferings, and this was in keeping with God's
character. " It became Him . . . to make the
Captain of their salvation perfect through sufferings " (verse 10). The correct reading in verse 10
is " *Having brought* " it is the aorist participle,
and speaks of the power of His supreme act of
suffering, in once for all dying, an act finished
and complete, the one righteousness, which con-
stitutes His children righteous and puts them into
glory. The word perfect or perfected when
applied to our Leader Christ must not be read as
if it means he had imperfections which required
righting. It is in no moral sense but is to be
read, in the sense of fitness or equipment. He
was fitted as man to lead men, by a pathway of
sufferings, consummated in the one supreme
atoning act on Calvary.

One has said, " The perfecting of Christ is the
leading of sons to glory. The leading of sons to

glory is the perfecting of Christ, and both together are the act of a moment." The verb perfect applied to Christ occurs in this epistle in the following passages, v. 9, vii. 28, translated consecrated. His perfect identification with His children is seen in birth, verse 14; in unity, verse 11; in worship, verse 12; and in a life of trust in God in verse 13. A true leader, indeed, Who Himself has trod the road, Who Himself has lived the life, One Who in every point was tempted like as they were, sin apart, and, therefore, is able to succour them that are tempted, verse 18.

His true humanity is told out in verse 14, " Forasmuch as the children are sharers in blood and flesh, he also himself in like manner partook of the same " (R.V.) It is interesting to note that the word for sharer (Koionoi) differs from the word used of Him rendered partook (Meteschon). The verb translated sharers is in the perfect. Having shared and continuing to share, but the verb partook is aorist, implying the one historic fact of the incarnation. Thus we see how God guards the humanity of His Son. The children were sharers, it was their common lot, apart from blood and flesh they had no previous existence. *Not so with Him*, He partook of same. He partook of it that He might die, and in dying bring to nought him that had the authority of death " and deliver them, who through fear of death were all their lifetime subject to bondage," verses 14, 15.

> " He Hell in hell laid low,
> Made sin He sin o'erthrew,
> Bowed to the grave destroyed it so
> And Death by dying shew."

This likeness to His brethren is absolutely essential to His priesthood. To be the death-taster, leader of God's sons, " serpent crusher," and High Priest of His people, He must become incarnate. He must be *man*. Not *a* man, but *man*, yea, " the Son of Man," the sum total of manhood, the true humanity of the race.

In verse 17, we read to make propitiation for the sins of " the people." Here and through the letter, " the people " mean *primarily* the Jewish people. God's ancient people. As High Priest He Himself will yet apply to that nation and people the full value of His atoning work. (*See* Daniel ix. 24.) We would close this great Chapter by beholding The Man. The one who brought His Godhead into our humanity, that He might in it give God in this guilty scene infinite pleasure, that in it He might die on behalf of every man, expiate sin, destroy the serpent, deliver from death, become a merciful and faithful High Priest, sympathise, succour, and save.

> " Hail Him the Virgin's Son,
> The God incarnate born,
> Whose arm alone the trophies won
> Which doth His brow adorn.
> Fruit of the mystic rose,
> True rod of Jesse's stem,
> The root from which all mercy flows,
> The Babe of Bethlehem."

ANALYSIS OF CHAPTER

Hebrews I.—Gold. His Deity.
Hebrews II.—The Shittim Wood. His Humanity.

THEME.
  1. The Great Salvation.
  2. The Great Saviour.

SALVATION.

1. God's final appeal, for *No Escape* if neglected.
2. By a " Son of Man " (Psa. viii.).
   (*a*) Suffering.
   (*b*) Dying.   } This, becoming God (v. 10).
   (*c*) Tempted.

A SON OF MAN.

1. Truly Human.
2. Partaker of our nature (v. 14).

   > *Note.*—" Likewise," *i.e.* in like manner, only here used in New Testament, meaning was born, ENTERED BY BIRTH.

THE WOMAN'S SEED.   (Gen. iii. 15).

THE " GOAL " REDEEMER OF " THE OLD TESTAMENT."

1. A Redeemer because a Kinsman.
2. An Avenger because a Redeemer.

EARTH'S SOVEREIGNTY GIVEN TO MAN (v. 5).

1. First Adam forfeited through sin. " We see not " (v. 8).
2. Last Adam. The man of Psalm 8.
3. The One Man, made a little lower than the angels. " We see Jesus " (v. 9).

CHRIST IN MANHOOD.

1. Heir of all things (Heb. i. 3).
2. His seed brought to glory (Heb. ii. 10).
3. Joint-heirs with Him (Rom. viii. 17).

THIS ADDED GLORY necessitates death. " He must die " (v. 19) to become

1. Death Taster (v. 9).
2. Leader of God's sons to glory (v. 10).

3. Sanctifier (v. 11).

    (*a*) By His death (Heb. x. 10).

    (*b*) By His present life and work (Ephes. v. 26, R.V.).

4. Serpent Crusher (v. 14).
5. Saviour (v. 16, R.V.).

    Taketh hold, *i.e.*, takes hold to save.

6. Succourer (v. 18).
7. High Priest ; Merciful and Faithful (v. 17).

KINSMAN REDEEMER (v. 14).

1. Takes our nature (sin apart) as His own for ever.
2. In it lived out His life here.
3. In it manifested the Father (Col. ii. 9).
4. In it made atonement.
5. In it ascended to the right hand of God.
6. In it brings all things into subjection.
7. In it crushes the serpent and is Himself bruised.
8. In it claims universal sovereignty over and worship from every creature.
9. In it lives and pleads now on " The Throne."

HUMANITY THUS EXALTED, Magnified and Glorified in the God Man.

" And did'st Thou love the race that loved not Thee ?
    And did'st thou take to Heaven a human brow ?
Dost plead with man's voice by the marvellous sea ?
    Art Thou our Kinsman now ?

O God, O Kinsman loved, but not enough !
    O Man, with eyes majestic after death !
Whose feet have trod along our pathways rough,
    Whose lips draw human breath !

By that one likeness which is ours and thine,
    By that one nature which doth hold us kin ;
By that high Heaven where, sinless, Thou dost shine,
    To draw us sinners in."

Superior and Supreme.

Chap. i. — Greater than Prophets. — My Sin-Purger.

,,   ii.—Greater than Angels.—My Captain and Serpent Crusher.

,,   iii.—Greater than Moses.—My Apostle and High Priest.

,,   iv.—Greater than Joshua.—My Saviour and Rest.

,,   v.—Greater than Aaron.—The Melchisedec Priest.

,,   vi.—Greater than Principles.—My Anchorhold and Forerunner.

,,   vii.—Greater than the Aaronic Priesthood.—My Surety.

,,   viii.—Greater than the Old Covenant.—My Minister, Mediator and Covenanter.

,,   ix.—Greater than all Levitical Sacrifices.—Himself their Substance.

,,   x.—Greater than the Great Atonement Offering and Tabernacle. — My Sanctifier and Perfecter.

,,   xi., xii.—Greater than all Faith's Heroes.—Himself, Faith's Author and Completer.

,,   xiii.—Greater than Judaism, in all its God-given Economy.—My Great Shepherd. Let us go forth to him.

> " Unto Thee, the homeless stranger—
>   Outside the Camp.
> Forth we hasten, fear no danger—
>   Outside the Camp.
> Thy reproach, far richer treasure
> Than all Egypt's boasted pleasure ;
> Drawn by love that knows no measure
>   Outside the Camp."

The words found in this Chapter, and nowhere else found in the New Testament, are :—

1. **Παραρρυωμεν**—pararruōmen, v. 1, translated "we should let them slip." Revisers, "we drift away." The revisers' italics give the literal meaning, "we drift away from them."

2. **μισθαποδοσιαν**—misthapodosian, v. 2, translated, "recompense." This word is also used in chaps. x. 35, xi. 26. It brings before us the judgment-seat of Christ, and raises the question of recompense there, pregnant with the most solemn possibilities, to which we do well to take heed.

3. **μερισμος**—merismos, v. 4, translated "gifts," but the revisers in their margin read "*Gr.* distributions." This word is also used in chap. iv. 12.

4. **συνεπιμαρτυρουντος**—sunepimarturountos, v. 4, translated "bearing *witness* with."

5. **Θελησιν**—thelēsin, v. 4, translated "will."

6. **Παραπλησιως**—paraplēsiōs, v. 14, translated "likewise." Revisers translate "in like manner." This was a great word with the early fathers in their defence of the true humanity of the Saviour.

7. **δηπου**—depou, v. 16. translated "indeed." While referring to this verse I would call your attention to the rendering in the revisers "For verily not of angels doth *He take hold*, but *He taketh hold* of the seed of Abraham.

The rendering in the authorised would lead you to understand that the application was to His incarnation, but this is not the thought. The verb "to take hold" (R.V.) means to take hold with the purpose of saving; see the same verb in Heb. viii. 9, and Matt. xiv. 31.

The thought is He laid not hold of angels to save them, but He laid hold of Abraham's seed to save them, please note Abraham's seed, not Adam's seed, remembering that we who believe are the sons of Abraham (Gal. iii. 7, 9.

Words Nos. 1, 3 and 5 are found in The Septuagint.

CHAPTER III

CHRIST—"GREATER THAN MOSES"

LIKE Chapter ii. this chapter opens with a parenthetical exhortation, "Wherefore, holy brethren, partakers of a heavenly calling, consider the Apostle and High Priest of our confession, even Jesus." "Holy brethren," holy not in their state and condition, for they had back-slidden and become such as have need of milk (Chapter v. 12), but holy in their standing in Christ (*see* Chapter ii. 11).

Consider, *i.e.*, contemplate Jesus as Apostle and High Priest. This consideration of Him is for very practical purposes. Not for mere knowledge which puffeth up, but for love which buildeth up. Here alone is the appellation "apostle" applied to Christ, *i.e.*, the sent one of His Father (John xx. 21). As Apostle He is the sent messenger of the Father to us, and as High Priest He has gone in for us to God, to exercise His priestly functions, for us Godward, for, note—If He be the apostle and High Priest, it is said to be of "*our* confession," even Jesus — here we have His human name, emphasising His true humanity as Apostle and priest, and thus we can contrast Him with Moses.

Moses was faithful in all God's house as a servant but Christ as a son. So in rank He is greater than Moses.

The "His house," in verses 2, 5 and 6, should be read "God's house" (*see* Margin of Revised). He

is greater than Moses for He is the builder of
the house, and, therefore, worthy of more honour
than the house. So our blessed Lord, as builder
of the house, is God (verse 4), and is greater than
that which He built, and more glorious than its
most faithful servant. How the Godhead of Jesus
shines out here for, as builder of all things, He
is God. The verb here translated builder implies
rather equipped or established. In Newbury's
version margin, " established or prepared " is given
as the Greek equivalent. It occurs elsewhere in
the letter (*see* ix. 2, 6 ; xi. 7). In the house
which Jesus equipped Moses was a faithful household servant for a testimony of those things which
were to be spoken after (verse 5). Moses testified
of Him, who as the sent one of the Father was
Himself the revealer of the Father, the complete
and final revelation of God. The ministry of
Moses was a transient ministry, he was only a
household servant, but the glorious person
" Christ " was a son, and " The Son abideth ever."
In verse 6 we come to a statement concerning
which there have been great disputings, viz.,
" Whose house are we, if we hold fast our boldness
and the glorying of our hope firm to the end."

The " if " is interpreted by some as conditional,
and leads them to treat the house here as a conditional house, and, indeed, not only here but also
in Heb. x. 21. Sure I am that such a thought is
unthinkable. The house here is a much wider
thing, thank God, than a company or companies
of saints scripturally gathered. *At least*, it contains the whole of the saved of this dispensation,
if, indeed, it is not a wider thing than that, contain-
ing the " all things " which God builded (verse 4).
The " if " is an " if " of argument, and in no way
suggests the house to be dependent on our obedi-

ence. Any more than the " if " in 1 Cor. xi. 2 and
Colossians i. 23 suggest that you may fall from
grace and be lost, or the " if " of Rom. viii. 31
makes God for His own a conditional thing.   No !
these " ifs " are all " ifs " of argument and not
condition.

But all those who would, through their interpretation of the " if," shut out of the House
here, the great mass of God's dear children, go
very very far beyond the text.   If *it is* conditional,
the conditons are expressly stated by God, thus,
" If we hold fast the confidence and the rejoicing
of the Hope firm unto the end," which every true
child of God surely does.   It all shows how easily
some can go far far beyond the word and bring
about to themselves and others untold sorrows.

In verse 8 we come to a very solemn warning
and exhortation.   It follows the statements as
to Christ's supremacy over Moses.   The warning
is illustrated by the wilderness experience of God's
people under Moses—God's house in the wilderness.   We have already in 1 Cor. x. 11, been told
that all these things happened to them for types,
and are written for our admonition, so we do
well to take heed.

It is a sad catalogue of failure and disaster,
but please note it did not *unhouse them* as some
would say, but it brought God's discipline upon
the people.   Forty years of hardening their hearts,
tempting, provoking, grieving, and proving God.
Ignorant of His ways and only seeing His acts,
and in consequence lost their entrance into Canaan,
and under the hand of God experienced death
in the wilderness.   The question of their souls'
salvation as we speak is not once raised.   It is a
question of a chastening at God's hands, for sin,
and a failing to enter the Canaan rest.   It is a

solemn example for us, for we too may so sin, hence the warning "Take heed, brethren, lest haply there shall be in any of you an evil heart of unbelief in falling away from the living God." "Falling away," here literally means "apostatising." It is a very solemn experience, that while moral delinquents are many and often restored, apostates are seldom ever restored. In verse 17 we read, "For we are become partakers with Christ, etc." It is not "*in Christ*" which is *standing*, but "*with* Christ" which is *state*. It is communion and fellowship, and not life (*see* John xiii. 8). "Thou hast no part *with* Me."

It is, indeed, a very solemn possiblity that this sad experience of God's people in the wilderness may be repeated in the church. Indeed, in 1 Cor. xi. 30 we find this word, "For this cause many among you are weak and sickly, and not a few sleep," surely here are carcases falling in the wilderness through disobedience. You have the same discipline suggested in John xv. 2, "Every branch in Me that beareth not fruit *He taketh it away.*" Also in Rev. ii. 23, where we find the Son of God saying, "And I will kill her children with death."

The questions of verses 16, 17 and 18 are solemn : For who ? And with whom ? Was it not with ? And to whom sware He ?

The number 40 is most suggestive. It is the number suggesting, testing and trying, and in the test they wickedly failed and provoked God, and lost the land of Canaan. Moses fell through disobedience. From Mount Nebo, on Pisgah's top, "The Lord showed him all the land," and all he saw was all he lost because of disobedience (Deut. xxxiv. 1). All this has its intensely solemn voice to us lest we through disobedience shipwreck the faith, miss the mark, and lose the reward, the enjoyment of it here, and its actual possession hereafter.

> " A little while ! 'Twill soon be past,
>   Why should we shun the shame and cross.
>   O let us in His footsteps haste
>   Counting for Him all else but loss.
>   O how will recompense His smile
>   The sufferings of this ' little while.' "

ANALYSIS OF CHAPTER

HOLY BRETHREN (v. 1).

1. *Holy* because of standing in Him (Heb. ii. 11 ; Eph. i. 4).
2. *Brethren* because of oneness with Him (Heb. ii. 11-14).

HEAVENLY CALLING (v. 1).

1. Heavenly in Character (John i. 13 ; iii. 3). " Born from Above " (Marg., R.V.).
2. Heavenly in Calling (Phil. iii. 14).
3. Heavenly in Citizenship—Politics (Phil. iii. 20).
4. Heavenly in Blessings (Eph. i. 3).
5. Heavenly in Position (Eph. ii. 6).
6. Heavenly in Testimony (Eph, iii. 10).
7. Heavenly in Warfare (Eph. vi. 12).
8. Heavenly in Weapons (2 Cor. x. 4, 5).
9. Heavenly in Destiny (John xiv. 1-3).
10. Heavenly in Glory (Col. iii. 4).

CONSIDER HIM (v. 1).

1. The Apostle.—Type, Moses (Exod. iii. 10).
                              Septuagint Version.
2. High Priest.—Type, Aaron.
3. Him being Faithful.—Who *is* Faithful (R.V.)
4. Jesus (R.V.).—His human Name.

c

GREATER THAN MOSES.

1. Greater in Rank.—" He, a Son."
2. Moses part of the House.
3. He is Creator and Builder of it.
4. Moses, Faithful as a Servant.
5. He, Faithful as a Son.
6. The Servant abideth not (John viii. 35).
7. The Son is Eternal (John viii. 35).
8. Moses, a Testimony of Coming Things.
9. Christ, the Subject of that Testimony.

OUR RELATIONSHIP TO HIM.

" Whose House are we ? " (v. 6).

ISRAEL'S WILDERNESS TRAGEDY.

Read Verses 7 to 11.

SOLEMN EXHORTATIONS.

1. Lest we so act (v. 13).
2. Lest we so suffer.

COMMANDS.

1. Harden not your heart (v. 8).
2. Take heed against unbelief (v. 12).
3. Exhort one another daily (v. 12).

LEST WE

1. Provoke God.
2. Tempt God.
3. Grieve Him.
4. Leave Him.
5. Harden our Hearts.
6. Hear not His Voice.
7. Enter not into His Rest.
8. Die Prematurely.

SOLEMN QUESTIONS (vv. 17, 18).

1. With whom was He grieved ?
2. To whom swear He that they should not enter into His rest ?

ANSWER.

1. Those whose carcases fell in the wilderness.
2. Those that were disobedient.

They failed to enter the Rest of Canaan.

We too may fail to enter into Rest (His Lordship Rest).

ENSAMPLES TO US, FOR

1. All went out of Egypt.
2. All were Baptised.
3. All did Eat of the Manna—Christ.
4. All did Drink of the Rock—Christ.

" Yet with many God was displeased, over-throwing them in the wilderness."

Words found in this Chapter and nowhere else in the New Testament :—

1. δοκιμασια—dokimasia (v. 9). Revisers, " in proving me."
2. Θεραπων—therapōn (v. 5), translated " a servant."
3. Παραπικρασμω — parapikrasmō (vv. 8, 15), translated " provocation."
4. Παρεπικραναν—Parepikranan (v. 16), translated " provoked."

All these words are found in The Septuagint.

CHAPTER IV

CHRIST—" GREATER THAN JOSHUA "

IN this Chapter we have a reference to Israel's
past and future history, and here again we need
to remember to whom this letter was sent. The
fact of past failure of those who went out of
Egypt is stated. The why ? of it is also stated.
They had the gospel preached to them, but the
word preached did not profit them, they not being
mixed by faith with them which heard (*i.e.*,
Joshua and Caleb). Then comes the solemn word
of warning, " Let us fear, therefore, etc. " The
rest preached was not heaven, but Canaan. They,
the nation, failed to enter in because of disobedience. Yet their remains a rest for the people
of God.

There is a reference in the Chapter to four rests :
1st. Creations ; 2nd. Canaan's Rest ; 3rd. Present
Rest, " We which have believed do enter into
rest (verse 3) ; and lastly, " There remaineth,
therefore, a *Sabbath Rest* for the people of God.
Even those who were obedient and went into the
land entered not into rest, " For if Joshua had
given them rest, then would He (God) not afterward have spoken of another day " (Psa. 110).
The promise of God is not made null and void by
the nation's disobedience, for it is still held out in
David. Therefore, there remaineth for that
people a *Sabbath rest* (R.V.) The word for rest
in verse 9 is different from the other word, trans-

lated Rest in the chapter; it is only found here, and means as the R.V. have translated it a "Sabbath rest," *i.e.* God's rest. *This rest* is more glorious than Canaan, and the rest of conscience now possessed by all who believe, for it is not only the rest God gives, but the rest God Himself enjoys, " God's own rest."

> " What will it be to dwell above,
>   And with the Lord of glory reign,
>   Since the blest knowledge of His love
>   So brightens all this dreary plain.
>   No heart can think, no tongue can tell
>   What joy 'twill be with Christ to dwell."

The whole argument proves that Israel never entered into God's rest, seeing the rest still remaineth and that the promise still abideth. The solemn exhortation is " Let us fear " (verse 1). Let us give diligence to enter into *" that rest "* that no man fall after the same manner of disobedience (verse 11). That we might not fail by the same manner of unbelief, we are commended to God and the word of His grace. The character and workings of God's " living word " are held up to faith's gaze, and faith's affections are directed to a " God man," who is alive at the right hand of God, and alive in our nature. One who *can be touched* with the feeling of our infirmities, tempted on all points, *sin apart*, as we are. Let us, therefore, hold fast our confession and come boldly to the throne of grace, that we may obtain mercy and find grace to help in time of need.

Please note He never knew the temptations of sin, for " He knew no sin," " had no sin," and " did no sin."

ANALYSIS OF CHAPTER

THEME.

1. God's Rest.
2. God's Word.
3. Our Great Priest.

REST.

1. Creations Rest in which God rested (v. 4).
2. Canaan's Rest (vv. 3 and 6).
3. Accepted by Faith (v. 2).
4. Rejected by Unbelief (v. 2).
5. Joshua's Failures (v. 8).
6. Preached by David (Psa. xcv. 7).
7. Entered Now by Faith (v. 3).
8. Yet in Time Partial (v. 8).
9. But in Eternity, Divinely Perfected (v. 9).

THE PEOPLE OF GOD.

Meaning God's Earthly People (primarily in every instance in Hebrews it is the Chosen People of God, Israel, that is under consideration.

1. Their Reconciliation (Heb. ii. 17 ; Dan ix. 24).
2. Their Rest (Heb. iv. 9).
3. In the Wilderness (Heb. v. 3).
4. Their Tithes (Heb. vii. 9).
5. Their Law (Heb. vii. 11 ; ix. 19).
6. Their Sins (Heb. vii. 27 ; ix. 7).
7. Their Covenant (Heb. viii. 10).
8. Their Judge (Heb. x. 30).
9. Their Bondage (Heb. xi. 25).
10. Their Sanctification (Heb. xiii. 12).

THE WORD OF GOD.

1. The Incarnate Word.
2. The Written Word.

> *For*   " The Scriptures and the Word
> Bear one tremendous Name,
> The Living and the Written Word
> In all things are the same."

THE WORD IS (Heb. iv. 12, 13).

1. Living.	5. Dividing.
2. Active.	6. Discerning.
3. Sharp.	7. Manifesting.
4. Piercing.	8. Stripping (Naked).

9. Lays open.   This is a sacrificial word which means (1) To press back the head ; (2) To bare the neck for the knife.

OUR GREAT HIGH PRIEST (vv. 14-16) (Aaron, " High " ; Christ, " Great ").

1. Himself the Sacrifice.
2. Divine (" Son of God ")—hence Great.
3. Human (Jesus)—so can be touched.
4. Tempted.   Therefore, " *Hold Fast.*"
5. Sinless—" Apart from Sin " (v. 15).
6. Accessible—" Able to be Touched."
7. Sympathetic—Feels our infirmities.

THE GOSPEL OF FREE ACCESS (v. 16).

1. Come Boldly.
2. Throne of Grace.
3. He gives Mercy and Grace.
4. Mercy—withholding what we do deserve.
5. Grace—imparting what we do not deserve.

" Let Us."

Let us also fear (chap. iv. 1).
Let us hold fast (chap. iv. 14).
Let us, therefore, draw near (chap. iv. 16).
Let us go on (chap. vi. 1).
Let us draw near (chap. x. 22).
Let us hold fast (chap. x. 23).
Let us consider (chap. x. 24).
Let us lay aside (chap. xii. 1).
Let us have grace (chap. xiii. 13).
Let us offer (chap. xiii. 15).
Let us, therefore, go forth (chap. xiii. 13).

Words found in this chapter, and nowhere else used in the New Testament :—

1. **σαββατισμος**—sabbatismos (v. 9), translated " rest." The revisers have translated it " Sabbath rest." It is not only future and eternal, but it is also " God's own rest." It remaineth for the people of God.

2. **ἁρμων**—harmon (v. 12), translated " joints." " Soul and spirit, joints and marrow," deal with the whole man (*see* 1 Thess. v. 23). Here it is the whole redeemed man subject to the searching power of God's living word.

3. **Τομωτερος**—tomōteros (v. 12), translated " sharper."

4. **διϊκνουμενος**—deknoumenos (v. 12), translated " piercing."

5. **Μυελων**—muelōn (v. 12), translated " *marrow*."

6. **αφανης**—aphanēs (v. 13), translated " not manifest."

7. **Τετραχηισμενα** — tetrachelismena (verse 13), translated " opened." *See* Analysis, *i.e.* A laying bare for the closest of scrutiny as to its fitness for sacrifice.

8. **συμπαθησαί**—sumpathesai (v. 15), translated " Be touched with the feeling of." Lit., to sympathise. This word is once again used in the epistle (*see* x. 4) ; where it is translated " compassion."

9. **ὁμοιότητα**—homoioteta (v. 15), translated " like." It is also used in chap. vii. 15.

Words Nos. 2, 4, 5, 6, 7, are found in The Septuagint.

CHAPTER V

CHRIST—"GREATER THAN AARON"

CHAPTER iv. 14 opens a section of the epistle which runs on to Chapter x. 22, and deals with the priesthood, sacrifice and ministry of our "Great High Priest." It opens with "Having then a Great High Priest, who hath passed through the heavens, Jesus the Son of God," and it closes with "and having a great priest over the house of God; let us draw near." We have seen Christ greater than prophets, angels, Moses and Joshua. Now we are asked to consider Him as greater than Aaron—greater in His manhood for He is "sin apart"—greater in His priesthood, for He is "The Son of God," a divine priest. He is perfectly human, for He is "Jesus." He is equally divine, for he is "The Son of God." True, He is not on earth as Aaron was, for He has passed through the heavens. Yea! He is higher than the heavens (Chapter vii. 26). Yet! He can be touched, and it is our privilege and responsibility as members of His priestly house, to follow Him there. Are we not thus exhorted in plain, simple language, such as: "Let us, therefore, draw near with boldness" (Chapter iv. 16); "Wherefore, He is able to save to the uttermost them that draw near" (Chapter vii. 25); "Let us draw near" (Chapter x. 22); "For he that cometh to God" (Chapter xi. 6). These scriptures clearly demonstrate our approach, yea! our *free access* into the innermost shrine of His abiding holiness and that, although billions of miles separate us physically, yet faith bridges the gulf and we can touch Him; yea! we can speak with Him face to face, and can express in our own souls what it is to live in the power of the gospel of free access. In our coming we will find there a priest. Nay! a *high* priest. Nay! a *great* high priest, Who, because He is perfectly human, can sympathise, and because He is divine can succour and save. His humanity is expressed in His human name, " Jesus." His Godhead is seen in the appellation, " The Son of God." One who was tested in every point like as we are, yet without sin; please note this should read " sin apart." He never knew the temptations of indwelling sin. This fact makes a vital difference between Him and us, between *all* His testings, and *most* of ours.

Chapter v. emphasises a great truth which has been before touched in Chapter ii. 17, viz., The divine necessity of true manhood for priesthood. First and foremost God's priest must be a real man, taken from among men, and appointed for men in things pertaining to God. The reason given for this is, " Who can bear gently with the ignorant and erring," " for that he himself also is compassed with infirmity " (verse 2).

Every legal high priest must offer for sin, for the people and also for himself. All this brings vividly before us the fact of the fall, that man is a sinner. If man had not fallen then no sacrifice would have been necessary, and if no sacrifice, then no priest, as a priest and a sacrifice are correlative terms. Aaron's very existence as priest was, that he might offer sacrifices for sins, that he might by the blood of a covenant victim bring near, and keep near, God's covenant people as cleansed worshippers. The manhood of the priest is essential to give the true human touch, the compassionate human heart, that only can impart true sympathy and compassion to all his priestly service. Hence God's high priest must be a man, this is a binding necessity, an irrevocable law. " *No man*," " *No priest.*" In verse 5 we are brought to Christ Himself. The Archetype and Antitype of the legal high priest for, as one has well said, " The priesthood and sacrifices of the law were not the original exemplar of these things, but a transcript and copy of what was done in heaven itself, in counsel, design, and covenant, as they were a type of what should afterwards be accomplished on earth " (Dewar on the Atonement). This quotation (Heb. viii. 5) fully warrants. It is a wonderful thought of which I may make fuller use when dealing with Chapter viii.

So also " The Christ glorified not Himself to be made a High Priest." I think here we must insist on translating the definite article before Christ and read it " The Christ." The high priest of Israel could not appoint himself, neither could any one else appoint him. He must be appointed by God. Which appointment honoured him (verse 4). So also " The Christ " glorified not Himself to become a high priest. The divine appointment honoured Aaron, but it *glorified* The Christ. In this He was greater than Aaron. Christ's call was based on His Sonship, " Thou art my Son, to-day have I begotten Thee." Hence again He is greater than Aaron, for He is a " Son ", not simply a servant. Yea! He is the Divine Priest. This is easily understandable for none save He, who is God, could sustain in humanity, such an office, for He *must be sacrifice* as well as priest (Heb. x. 5-9) " Thou art my son, to-day have I begotten Thee." This is a quotation from Psalm ii. It is also found in Chapter i. 5. The difficulty is in the phrase " To-day have I begotten Thee." What is meant by " To-day." Origon and St Augustine, also Plato and others, insist on "To-day," being "God's Eternal Day," and make it apply to what is called by the fathers, " The Eternal Generation of the Son." Bishop Pearson writes, "Christ has a four-fold right to the title ' Son of God ' — I. By eternal generation ; II. By incarnation ; III. By resurrection as the First-born from among the dead ; and IV. By universal and actual possession as Heir of all things."

I think the passage here must refer to resurrection (see Acts xiii. 33 ; Romans i. 4.) Both these passages, I know, are disputed as referring to the resurrection of Christ. A very fanciful interpretation is put on Acts xiii. 33, based on the absence of " again " as not in the original, and Romans i. 4 is rejected because " spirit of holiness " has not the article, but with all deference to those who so dispute, I still hold fast, with countless others, to the good old interpretation, viz., His resurrection from among dead ones.

In Hebrews v. 5-6, the quotation from Psalm ii., and also from Psalm cx., answers to His call and appointment to His priesthood, which glorified Him. Most suggestive are these two quotations, Greater than Aaron for He is an Eternal Being, " The Son of God," and greater because He is a priest *for ever*, and not only for ever, but also after the order of Melchisedec. Verses 7 and 8, tell us some things which happened in the days of His flesh which we do not get in the gospels, viz., He wept for Himself, etc., Note verse 8 should read " out of death." This refers to the scene in

Gethsemane, if, indeed, it does not include Calvary. He was heard because of His piety. "Son though He were," yet learned He obedience by the things which He suffered; please note it is not said He learned to obey, but He learned obedience; of course this could only apply to "*the days of His flesh*," to His true and dependent manhood. His cryings and tears, His obedience and surrender to the will of His Father, the "not My will but Thine be done" was all in the lesson of obedience. Such a sight had never before been witnessed by God or man. A true man in perfect submission to His father's will, and whose only desire was that will. His praying and obeying went together. Note the obedience is not learned from His sonship but from His *suffering*. And being made perfect, He became the author of eternal salvation to all them that obey Him. Then in resurrection. "Saluted by God, High Priest after the order of Melchisedec." For the use of the word eternal in the epistle (*see* Analysis of Chapter xiii). Having introduced Melchisedec as the Order of Christ's Priesthood, he wanted to say many things and hard to be uttered, difficult because of their spiritual condition, for they had become such as had need of milk and not meat, and had become dull of hearing. So from Chapters v. 13 to vi. 19 we have a parenthetical exhortation to go on to full manhood. A manhood that, by reason of use, has its senses exercised to discern good and evil.

ANALYSIS OF CHAPTER

THEME : *The Priesthood of Christ.*
TYPE : " *Aaron.*" " *Melchisedec.*"
   (*Chapter* begins *Section* ending Heb. x. 18.)

1. HIS MANHOOD. Essential. (v. 1.)
   Taken from among men (Heb. ii. 17).
2. HIS GODHEAD. " Thou art My *Son* " (v. 5).
3. HIS COMPASSION (v. 2).
   Compassion here is a distinct word from
   chap. iv. 15, and means " *moved to emotion.*"
4. HIS ORDER. Melchisedec (v. 6).
5. HIS SACRIFICE. " Once for all," *i.e., absolute, final*, hence. Chap x. 10.
6. HIS SALVATION. Eternal (v. 9).
7. PERFECTED. Through obedience and suffering (vv. 8, 9). (Heb. ii. 10.)
8. LIKE HIS BRETHREN. " Days of His flesh " (v. 7). (Heb. ii. 17.)

> " Whose feet have trod our pathways rough,
>   Whose lips draw human breath."

Called by God (v. 4).

CHRIST GREATER THAN AARON

Contrasts :
   Aaron's call *honoured* him (v. 4).
   Christ's call *glorified* Him (v. 5).
   Aaron called from among *the living* (v. 1).
   Christ called from among *the dead* (v. 5, *see* chap. viii. 4), " To-day have I begotten Thee," *i.e.*, His resurrection.
   Aaron made without an *oath* (Heb. vii. 21).
   Christ with an *oath* (Heb. vii. 20).
   Aaron called a *man*, compassed with infirmity (v. 2).
   Christ called a *Son*, perfected for evermore (Heb. vii. 28).
   Aaron's consecration *partial*, and for time (Exod. 28).

Christ's consecration *complete* and *eternal* (Heb.
vii. 28).

Aaron's holiness *symbolical*.

Christ's holiness *literal*.

Aaron's atonement *typical*.

Christ's atonement *actual*.

Aaron a priest by and for *continual* sacrifices.

Christ a Priest by a " *once for all* " *sacrifice* (Heb.
x., 11, 12).

Aaron a sinner *needing* a sacrifice (chap. v. 1).

Christ, " that holy thing," *giving* Himself a
Sacrifice (Heb. ix. 14).

Aaron enters by blood of *others*.

Christ enters by *His own* blood (Heb. ix. 12).

GREATER THAN AARON.

1. *In Rank*, a Son, Divine (v. 8).
2. *In Manhood*, no sin, no infirmity (chap. vii.
   28).
3. *In His Sacrifice*, His own blood (chap. ix. 12).
4. *In Results*, " Having obtained eternal salvation " (v. 9).
5. *In His Priesthood*, eternal, not transferable
   (Chap. vii. 24).
6. *In His Order*, " after the order of Melchisedec " (v. 10).
7. *Saluted by God* (v. 10). Word "called"
   here is only used in this passage and means
   " saluted." (*See* Psa. ii. 6, " The setting of
   the King " ; Psa. cx. 1, " The setting of Him,
   the Priest.")

CHRIST'S MANHOOD. Real. Very Man.

1. *A Suffering Manhood*. " Strong cryings and
   tears " (v. 7).
2. *A Sinless Manhood*. " Sin apart " (chap. iv.
   15).

(*a*) Had no sin.
(*b*) Knew no sin (2 Cor. v. 21).
(*c*) Did no sin (1 Peter—ii. 22).
(*d*) Would not sin.

3. *God's Relationship to Him.*   " His Father."
4. *Obedience Learned* (v. 8).   Only possible in manhood.
5. *He Perfectly Obeyed* (Phil. ii. 8) ; and
6. *He Trusted* (Heb. ii. 13).
7. *Prayed and Supplicated* (v. 7), Gethsemane.
8. *Heard for His piety* (v. 7), in that He feared, *i.e.*, for His piety.
9. *Saved from Death* (v. 7), *i.e.*, out of death.

   (*a*) Calvary.
   (*b*) Resurrection.

GREAT WORDS OF THE EPISTLE—" *Better*."

1. Better than angels (chap. i. 4).
2. Better hope (chap. vii. 19).
3. Better covenant (chap. viii. 6).
4. Better promises (chap. viii. 6).
5. Better sacrifices (chaps. ix., xxiii).
6. Better substance (chap. x. 34).
7. Better country (chap. xi. 16).
8. Better resurrection (chap. xi. 35).
9. Better things (chap. xii. 24).

THEME.   " *Melchisedec*."

SUBJECT.

1. Many things to say.   Section chap. v. 11 ; to chap. x. 18.
2. Hard of Interpretation (v. 11).

WHY ?   Because of backsliding (vv. 11, 13).
   Parenthesis.   Chap. v. 11 to Chap. vi. 23.

D

APPOSITIONS (vv. 11-13).
1. " Babes "—" Men."
2. " Milk "—" Solid food."
3. " Babes "—" Teachers."
4. " Without experience " — " By reason of use."

EXERCISE (*i.e., Gymnastics*—see only use in N.T.)
(*a*) Exercise of body (1 Tim. iv. 8).
(*b*) Exercise of senses (Heb. v. 14).
(*c*) Exercise of suffering (Heb. xii. 11).
(*d*) Exercise of covetousness (2 Pet. ii. 14).

List of Words found in this Chapter, and nowhere else used in the New Testament :—
1. **ευλαβειας**—eulabeias (v. 7), translated " feared. Revisers translate it " Godly fear." This word is used in the epistle once again, Chap. xii. 28 ; there the revisers translate it " Awe." I think the R.V. have truly translated it by " Godly fear."
2. **εκετηριας**—eketērias (v. 7), translated " prayers."
3. **αιτιος**—aitios (v. 9), translated " author." Revisers margin have *Gr.* Cause ; this is the better translation.
4. **Προσαγορευθείς**—prosogorutheis (v. 10), translated " called." The revisers give " named." The Newberry Bible gives " addressed." The Englishman's Greek New Testament gives " *Having been saluted*." This latter rendering I believe gives the best translation. What lovely and glorious thoughts this word causes to arise in our hearts ! God saluting as high priest in resurrection, His glorious and triumphant *Son* (*see* Psa. cx.) ! Jehovah addressing His fellow !

5. **νωθρος**—nothros (v. 11), translated "dull." This word is also used in chap. vi. 12, where it is translated "slothful." The R.V. there translating it "*Sluggish*."

6. **επειρος**—epeiros (v. 13), translated "unskilful." Revisers translate "without experience."

7. **ἑξιν**—exin (v. 14), translated "use." The thought is better expressed by "Habit."

8. **αισθχτηρια**—aisthētēria (v. 14), translated "senses." I suppose the word must here stand for spiritual senses. These so trained by reason of habit to discern *both* good and evil.

Words Nos. 1, 2, 3, 5, 6, 7, 8 are found in The Septuagint.

CHAPTER VI

" FULL GROWTH "

CHRISTIAN MANHOOD

IN Chapter v. 11, the apostle expresses his difficulty in writing concerning " Melchisedec " of
whom he had many things to say, and hard to be
uttered, because of their spiritual condition. The
wonderful truths bound up in Melchisedec were
such, that only men of maturity, men of full
growth, could receive and appreciate. They
called for men, skilful men, who by reason of use
had their senses exercised (*i.e.*, trained) to discern
both good and evil. These Hebrews to whom he
wrote ought, by reason of age in Christ, to have
been men and teachers, but alas ! they had
become dull of hearing, and also had *become* such
as had need of milk and not of strong meat. In
other words they had back-slidden and failed to
go on. Chapter vi., an exhortation to go on to
full-growth. The Greek word translated perfection, means " full-growth," or " maturity."
See its other usages in the New Testament, for the
study of it is most helpful. These Hebrews, alas !
are not alone in this sad condition. How many
Christians has one met who, because of the many
years of their Christian life, should be strong,
alert in hearing, and able to discern the deep
things of God, yet they are still babes ! To
all such this exhortation comes, " Let us go on
unto full-growth," and not be ever relaying the
foundations and in a constant state of flux,

wondering if this and that are really so or not.
Leave the first principles of the doctrine of Christ
and go on, is God's exhortation. A tree must
leave its roots, a building its foundations, and a
a saint must not spend his precious life in baby-
hood, laying and relaying foundations, all important as these foundations are. The foundations
are distinctly named. They are—

> " Repentance from dead works.
> Faith toward God.
> The doctrine of washings and laying on of hands.
> The Resurrection of the dead.
> And of Eternal Judgment."

The Jew, unlike the Gentile, had all this previous fundamental training. Privileged, indeed,
but in danger of resting there; even after his
acceptance of Christ and his embracing of Christianity, he was in constant danger of "laying
again," and going back, and not going onward up
to full manhood. The "Let us go on," of verse is
really "Let us be borne along," and at once
emphasises the necessity of the work of God the
Holy Spirit in our spiritual development and
growth. The Hebrew was in danger of forgetting
that the law was simply a schoolmaster to Christ,
essential in their state as infants, but to be left
behind in their development as Sons (*see* Gal. iv.)
All these specified foundations were in and be-
longed to, the teaching of Judaism. Now that
they had accepted Christ, God says "Let us go
on."

In verses 4-6 we have a much debated and
disputed portion. Calvin, in order to maintain
the eternal security of the true believer, argues
that those mentioned here, are professors, and
not possessors, while those who believe in the
" falling away " doctrine use the passage to support

their peculiar tenets. I would here say that all this confusion and difficulty is not in the passage at all, but is read into it. God does not say it is impossible to renew *any one* again unto repentance. What the passage does say is this, " It is impossible to renew them again unto repentance, *while* they crucify afresh the Son of God and put Him to an open shame " (*see* Margin of Revised). The emphasis is on the verb, translated *seeing*, which is in the present participle, and must be read, " while they are." It is a case of " Cease to do evil, and learn to do well." " The falling away " of verse 5 has no reference whatever to moral evil. The delinquent here is not a moral backslider, but is an " *Apostate*." The evil is spiritual. It is a renunciation of the full, clear and final revelation of God in His Son, and a going back to the beggarly elements of Judaism. It was a state into which the early Hebrew believers were liable and very prone to fall. The whole letter was written to save them from this. Do you wonder at this constant Hebrew besetment ? Judaism was of divine origin. Its ordinary ritual, sacrifices and constitution were *wholly* divine. Prior to His crucifixion it was the only acknow-ledged system on earth ; of it we read, " Who are Israelites, to whom pertaineth the adoption, and the glory and the covenants and the giving of the law, and the service of God, and the promises." " Whose are the fathers and of whom as concern-ing the flesh, Christ came " (Rom. ix. 4-5). These Hebrews were just men like ourselves. How many of God's people have we met and known, who have judged systems of religion around to be unscriptural and contrary to the mind of God and therefore have come out, yet afterward, for reasons best known to themselves, have been

allured into them again and are found building
again the things they once destroyed, and thus
constituting themselves transgressors (Gal. ii. 18).

The apostate here is a supposed case, and not
an actual one, for please note verse 9, " But
beloved we are persuaded better things of you
and things that accompany salvation though we
thus speak." The " crucifying to themselves afresh
the Son of God," and " putting Him to an open
shame," (verse 6) ; is a condition peculiar to *this*
apostacy. It is a going back to Jewish altars and
sacrifices. Indeed, to be so guilty demands an
altar and a sacrifice. The right interpretation of
this passage depends on our carefully reading the
address on the envelope of the letter, viz., " To
the Hebrews." The description given by God in
verses 4 and 5 in the experience of a Hebrew does
not of necessity demand true and genuine salvation. I suggest that the conditions of believing
Hebrews described in Acts xxi. 20-28, explains
the meaning of the descriptions of verses 4 and 5 ;
and I am satisfied that many of those there
could be thus described, and yet not be genuinely
converted to God at all. The apostacy of this
Hebrew letter was of the most appalling character. It was the renunciation of Jesus as the
true Messiah. It was an agreement with His
mock trial and ignominious death. It was a
revival of the cry, " Away with Him ! Away
with Him ! " etc. It was truly a crucifixion of
the Son of God and the putting of Him to an
open shame.

The whole of this portion is a solemn warning
from God against not only apostasy, but a continuance therein. There is not only the terrible
nature of its sin, *i.e.*, " Crucifying afresh the
Son of God, and putting Him to an open shame,"

but verses 7 and 8 show the terrible consequences, even if repented of, of the sin—a life wrecked, a life lost. It brings prominently to the front the judgment seat of Christ, the testing of the life here, as to what of it has borne fruit that will eternally abide. How much of it will be saved, how much of it will provide fuel for the flames and be burnt up ?   Life is too short and the salvation of the soul too precious to have any part of it lost at the judgment seat.

Note in verse 7, " the oft upon it," emphasises God's long suffering and tender mercies.

For them by whom it is dressed can only refer in its application to our God, who has said, " Ye are God's husbandry " (1 Cor. iii. 9), *i.e.*, God's tillage or cultivated field. He dresses it, He blesses it. He looks for and expects fruit ; " by whom it is dressed " should read for whom it is dressed, *i.e.*, *For its owner*. But, alas ! what a terrible calamity when these lives of ours, so graciously blessed and tended by their owner, should only yield a crop which in the testing day will not add to the granary of God, but to the flames of the fire. This portion is, indeed, solemn, *primarily* true of the Hebrew, in principle—true of any true believer.

The apostle was, however, persuaded better things of the Hebrew saints and things which accompany salvation (verse 9). Here salvation must be taken in its broadest and fullest meaning. God's great salvation, which finds us poor sinners at the Cross, saves, and continues to save, right on to the glory, including not only our salvation as *sinners*, but also our salvation as *saints*. In verses 10-12 we have words of encouragement spoken reminding them of the faithfulness and righteousness of God, and exhorting to diligence, hope, faith and endurance, right on to the end, an end made sure to us by the two immutable things of God, His oath and His word. These give to us a strong consolation, lifting our hearts to the great anchor hold, Himself. Jesus the forerunner, entered into the holy of holies, and entered for us, made an high priest for ever after the order of Melchisedec. This wonderful chapter ends with a taking up again of the great theme left in Chapter v. 10, and in Chapter vii. he goes on to unfold the great truths of this King-priest, setting forth the fulfilment of the type in Jesus, the forerunner.

ANALYSIS OF CHAPTER

THEME.—Pressing on to full manhood.

EXHORTATIONS—*Leave.*

1. " The word of the beginning of Christ "
   (chap. vi. 1).
2. As a building leaves its foundations.
3. As a tree its roots.
4. As a man his childhood.
5. It is the leave of growth, of development.
   Go on to Full Growth—
   (*a*) Manhood.   (*b*) Solid food.

FOUNDATIONS TO LEAVE (vv. 1, 2).

1. Repentance.	4. Laying on of hands.
2. Faith.	5. Resurrection of the dead.
3. Baptisms.	6. Eternal judgment.

PROOFS OF A SPIRITUAL EXPERIENCE (vv. 4-6).

   (*a*) Enlightened.
   (*b*) Tasted of the Heavenly Gift.
   (*c*) Partaker of Holy Spirit.
   (*d*) Tasted the good Word of God.
   (*e*) Tasted the Powers of the Coming Age.

SOLEMN WARNING (vv. 6-8).

1. Having fallen away (*Apostatised*).
2. Impossible to renew again to repentance
3. While crucifying afresh the
4. Son of God, and putting Him
5. To an open shame.

> *Note.*—God does not say it is *impossible* to renew again to *repentance*, but it is impossible to renew again to *repentance* while they are doing this. This is the force of the tense of the verb (*see* R.V.). The evil is not *moral*, but *spiritual*. It is a going back to Judaism, requiring an *altar* and a *victim* on it. One of the proofs that the epistle was written while the temple was standing (*see* also chap. xiii. 10).

Yet Only a Warning (*see* v. 9).

FULL ASSURANCE (v. 11). (Word only used four times in New Testament.)

1. With the Mystery (Col. ii. 2).
2. With the Gospel (1 Thess. i. 5).
3. With the Hope (Heb. vi. 11).
4. With our Approach to God (Heb. x. 22).

GOD'S OATH (v. 17). God stooping to man's level and confirming His promise by an oath. *Delitzch.* Interposed or mediated by an oath (*Gk.*).

PERJURY IMPOSSIBLE. Impossible for God to lie (v. 18).

THE HOPE.

1. *" Sure."   " Steadfast."   " Entering."*
2. Anchor of the soul.
3. Its anchorage.
4. The *" Forerunner."   " Jesus."   " Melchisedec."*
5. Within the vail.

> *Note.*—In every usage of the Hope in Hebrews (chaps. iii. 6 ; vi. 11, 18, 19 ; vii. 19 ; x. 23) it is the Hope of Entrance, not the Hope of His Coming. It is not the Hope that comes out, but the Hope that goes in.

MELCHISEDEC. He thus closes his parenthesis of *Exhortation* and *Warning*, where he left off in chapter v. 10, viz., with *Melchisedec*, and now goes on to say " The *Many Things* difficult to understand."

The following list of words in this Chapter are only found here in the New Testament :—

1. αναστavρουνταϛ—anastaurountas (v. 6), translated " seeing they crucify." The revisers in their margin have " The while " they crucify. The tense of the verb is the present participle, implying a continuance in the apostacy. While this state continues repentance is impossible. The final continuance in this course would prove that the person so doing had never been saved at all, simply a professor.

2. Παραδειγματιζονταϛ.—paradeigmatizontas (v. 6), translated " put Him to an open shame.'

3. Βοτανην—botanēn (v. 7), translated " herbs."

4. Γεωργειται—Geōrgeitai (v. 7), translated " it is dressed." Revisers give " tilled."

5. Καυσιν—Kausin, translated " burning."

6. **'α·μεταθετον**—ametatheton (vv. 17 and 18), translated "immutable."

7. **εμεσιτευσεν**—emesitusen (v. 17), translated "confirmed." The revisers give "interposed," and in their margin (*Gk.* mediated). He interposed Himself by means of an oath.

8. **Προδρομας.**—prodromas (v. 20), translated "forerunner."

Words Nos. 1, 2, 3, 4, 5, 8 are found in The Septuagint.

CHAPTER VII

CHRIST—GREATER THAN THE LEVITICAL PRIESTHOOD

WE have now come to the great and central Chapter of the epistle. Christ a priest for ever after the order of Melchisedec. To a Hebrew, the great difficulty was, how could Christ be a priest at all, seeing He was of Judah's tribe and not Levi's ? a tribe of which no man gave attendance at the altar. Had not one of its best kings attempted to do so, and did not God strike him with leprosy for doing so ? To meet this truly genuine difficulty, the writer lays hold of the Melchisedec type or order of priesthood. In studying this most interesting theme, let us ever keep before our mind that while, the *order* is Melchisedec, the pattern is Aaron.

The first eleven verses are descriptive of this mysterious man Melchisedec. He comes on the scene for the first time in Genesis xiv., is not heard of again for a thousand years (Psalm cx.), and then is lost sight of for another thousand years and turns up in Hebrews v. Some say he was Seth, others say that he was Christ Himself in one of " The Theophanies."

That he was a Canaanite is clear, but not Seth. That he was of necessity a real man is also clear, else he could not have been a priest at all, for *true* manhood is essential to priesthood (Heb. v. 1) ; while " The Theophanies " were a manifestation of God in *human* form, they were not *true* manhood. That he was not " The Son of God," is surely made clear by Hebrews vii. **3**, " *made like* unto the Son of God, abideth a priest continually."

God is speaking of Melchisedec, not as a man, but officially as a king and priest. The historic record of this man in Genesis xiv. 18-20 is remarkable, not only for what it says, but also for what *it does* not say. In recording it, God gave every word, and so worded it with a view to its use as the type of the coming great priest over " The house of God." To the writer of the record in Genesis. It is as if God says, " just say what is said and no more." So he comes before us a king and priest without a pedigree, having no recorded genealogy. Fatherless, motherless, birthless, and deathless. A priest not by succession, but in his own right. The first of his kind and the last of his kind. *Never one* before him, *never one* after him. " Made *like* unto the Son of God, abideth a priest continually (v. 3)."

The greatness of this man and order is seen in a sevenfold way :—

1. He blessed Abram who had the promises, " and without all contradiction the less is blessed of *the greater* " (verses 6, 7).

2. He tithed Abram. Levi had a commandment to take tithes of his brethren, but here is one who *tithed* Abram, and not only Abram, but Levi, for he was still in the loins of his father when Melchisedec met him (verses 9, 10) ; and not only so, in tithing Abram, he tithed *Humanity* ; for of Abram it is said, " In thee shall all families of the earth be blessed "—and in like manner in blessing Abram he blessed

humanity, and the tense of the verb "blessed," is such that the blessing is looked upon as still abiding (verses 6, 7).

3. " And here men that die, receive tithes, but there, he received them, of whom it is witnessed that he liveth."

4. Levi is seen paying tithes to Melchisedec, proving the order to be *prior* and *greater* than the Levitical priesthood.

5. The order of Melchisedec is seen setting aside the whole Levitical order and its legal base, as weak, unprofitable, and perfecting nothing (verses 11, 19).

6. Aaron was made priest without an oath, but Melchisedec *with an oath*, by Him that said unto Him, " The Lord sware and will not repent, thou art a priest for ever after the order of Melchisedec (verse 21). Note the oath of an eternal God *must be* an Eternal oath.

7. The Melchisedec order is untransmitable. It passes not to another. " And they were many priests because they were not suffered to continue by reason of death. But this man because he *continueth* ever, hath an unchangeable priesthood " (verse 24).

These seven points are unmistakeable proofs of the *greatness* of Christ's order over that of Aaron's The Aaronic order had no perfecting powers. " It made nothing perfect." Its Base, the law was weak and unprofitable, hence the necessity of another kind of priest to arise the blood of whose " once for all sacrifice " would " *purge for* ever," " *sanctify for* ever," and " *perfect for* ever." One who, because He liveth, ever could save to the uttermost, all coming to God through Him. One who could *bring us to God*.

The historic record of Melchisedec in Genesis xiv., presents him as a priest in benediction. There is no altar, no sacrifice, simply revealing and blessing, and so ministering, that Abram is *kept from falling*. What a beautiful type of our Lord's *present* session at God's right hand. We have said Melchisedec does not come before us as a sacrificing priest with an altar and sacrifice, for a sacrificing priest *to-day* would be a denial of Calvary.

This new order demanded a change of *law, tribe, sanctuary* and *priest*. Aaron is seen a sinful man, compassed with infirmity, offering continuously sin offerings for himself and the people which never did, nor could, take away sins or perfect the worshipper or bring him to God. All the Levitical ritual rested on a law, weak and imperfect (verses 18, 19), a law that perfected nothing. Their ordination was by a *carnal* commandment (verses 16, 20). Their sanctuary was only *ceremoniously* clean. Their sacrifices were *unintelligent, unwilling, protesting* victims, forced into it against their will. The *eternal* oath of an *eternal* God could not possibly be associated with an imperfect priesthood like this, and so we read, "if, therefore, perfection were by the Levitical priesthood, for under it (upon it) the people received the law, what further need was there that another priest should rise after the order of Melchisedec, and not be called after the order of Aaron" (verse 11)? The priest of this new order "Our Lord" became a priest not after the law of a carnal commandment, but after the *power* of an *endless* life (verse 16). Note the great contrast first between law and power, and secondly between a carnal (*i.e.*, fleshly) commandment and an "*in-dissoluable* life." The margin of the revised has for endless, "*indissoluble*." This word is peculiar to this verse, and is nowhere else found in the New Testament. This settles for ever the vexed question so often raised, namely, "when did Christ's priesthood begin?" This word "*in-dissoluble* life" determines it. It must be posterior to Calvary, death must not and cannot intervene. It establishes the fact that our Lord entered on His priestly work in resurrection (*see* Heb. v. 5-10). It is the "better hope" (verse 19) by which we draw nigh to God. The Gospel of *free access* of "perfected for ever-worshippers."

We see Him also in verse 22 as "*the surety*" of a "better covenant." The word translated "surety" is only found here, in the New Testament, and is also absent from the Septuagint. As their "surety," or "covenant victim," He deals with their sins. As their *great high priest* He brings them to God.

The *for* of verse 26 completes the argument by emphasising the spiritual fitness of our Lord for this great office. Not one who was only typically and ceremonially clean and holy, but *one* who is *actually* and *perfectly* so. "For such an high priest became us, holy, harmless, undefiled, separate from sinners, and made higher than the heavens" (verse 26). Revised Version reads "*separated* from sinners," *i.e.*, removed beyond every possibility of assault—"Holy" Godward, "harmless," manward, "undefiled" inward, Our Holy Lord! Now for the first time in the letter we are brought *distinctly* and *definitely* to His sacrifice, which was Himself. *Once for* all, as it must of necessity be, and therefore eternally efficacious, for all in the covenant. The Chapter finishes with the great contrast between Christ and Aaron. *The law*

E

maketh men high priests who have *infirmity*, but the word of the *Oath* which was since the law (Psa. cx. 4) maketh a son, who is *perfected for evermore* (verse 28). We gather from this great Chapter that our Lord is a priest for ever after the order of Melchisedec, exercising His priestly functions on our behalf to save us from falling (v. 25), while Christ as our " *advocate* " (1 John ii. 1), is seen pleading on behalf of a sinning saint. *So !* the more we know of His power in our hearts and lives as " Melchisedec," the less we will need to know of Him as our " Advocate." Let us see to it then, that our habit of life may be " them that are coming to God through Him." For if we thus prove the " coming ones " He will surely prove the " saving one," ministering to us the bread that strengthens and the wine that cheers, so that Abram-like we may overcome, and be more than conquerors, through Him that loves us.

ANALYSIS OF CHAPTER

TYPE.—Melchisedec " made like " (v. 3).

CONTRAST.—Aaron (v. 11).

VERSES 1-3.

1. Melchisedec, *i.e.*, King of Righteousness.
2. Salem, *i.e.*, King of Peace.
3. A king-priest.
4. Priest of the Most High God (v. 1 ; Gen. xiv. 18).
5. Righteousness and peace united in Him (Isa. xi. 5).
6. Tithed Levi. Greater than Aaron and *Wider* than the *Nation* (v. 9).

7. Without father without mother.
8. Without descent.
9. Without beginning of days.
10. Without end of life.
11. Abideth a priest continually.

GREATER THAN AARON.

1. His rank, " Son of God " (v. 3).
2. His Priesthood, perfect and perfecting (vv. 11, 18).
3. His order, " Melchisedec " (Zech. vi. 13).
4. His constitution, " the power of an endless life " (v. 16).
5. His tribe, " Judah." Regal (v. 15).
6. His ability, " To save to the uttermost " (v. 25).
7. His Priesthood, " Eternal " (v. 21).
8. Constituted by an Oath (v. 21).

HIS FITNESS.

1. *In Character.*
    (*a*) " Holy."   Godward. ⎫
    (*b*) " Harmless." Manward. ⎬ (v. 26)
    (*c*)   Undefiled. Inward. ⎭
2. *In Position.*
    " Separated from sinners " (R.V.).   Placed beyond the reach of assault.
3. *His Sacrifice.*
    " Himself " (vv. 22-27).   " Once for all," Eternal.

Words found in this Chapter, and nowhere else used in the New Testament:—

1. αγενεαλογητος—agenealogētos (v. 3), translated " without descent." Revisers translate " without genealogy."

2. **απατωρ**—apatōr (v. 3), translated "without father."

3. **διηνεκες**—diēnekes (v. 3), translated "continually." This word is also found in chaps. x. 1 ; xii. 14. In the Greek it is found with eis, and is translated "in perpetuity."

4. **αμητωρ**—amētōr, translated "without mother."

5. **δεηατην**—dekatēn (vv. 2, 4, 8, 9), translated "tenth," "tithes."

6. **ακροθινίων**—akrothiniōn (v. 4), translated "spoils." This word really means "the best of the spoils."

7. **αφωμοιωμενος**—aphōmoiōmenos (v. 3), translated "made like." This word is God's refutation of the statement one often hears, viz., "that Melchisedec was the Son of God."

8. **γενεαλογουμενος** — genealogoumenos (v. 6), translated "descent." Revisers give "Genealogy."

9. **δεδεκατωκεν**—dedekatoken (vv. 6, 9), translated "received tithes."

10. **νενομοθετητο**—nenomothetēto (v. 11), translated "received the law." Also used in chap. viii. 6.

11. **ιερωσυνης**—ierōsunēs (vv. 11, 12, 14, 24), translated "priesthood."

12. **μεταθεσίς**—metathesis (v. 12), translated "a change." This word is also found in chap. xi. 5, where it is translated "was translated."

13. **Καταδηλον**—katadēlon (v. 15), translated "evident."

14. **ὁμοιοτητα**—homoiotēta (v. 15), translated "similitude." This word is also found in chap. iv. 15.

15. **Ἀθετησὶς**—athetēsis (v. 18), translated " dis-
annulling." This word is also found in chap.
ix. 26, where it is translated " put away."

16. **επεὶσαγωγη**—epeisagōgē (v. 19), translated
" bringing in."

17. **ὀρκωμοσίας**—horkōmosias (vv. 20, 21, 28),
translated " oath."

18. **εγγνος**—enguos (v. 22), translated " surety."

19. **απαραβατον**—aparabaton (v. 24), translated
" unchangeable." Revisers in their margin
say " a priesthood that does not pass to
another," the *Gk.* is intransmissable.

The words Nos. 3, 6, 9, 10, 11, 12, 13, 14, 15, 16,
17, 18, 19, are all found in The Septuagint
version.

CHAPTER VIII

CHRIST—HIS MORE EXCELLENT MINISTRY

THIS Chapter opens with the "sum-all," "crown-all," or pith of what has gone before. "We have such an High Priest, who is set on the right hand of the throne of the majesty of the heavens. A minister (*i.e.* public minister) of the sanctuary and true tabernacle which the Lord pitched and not man."

> "No temple made with hands
> His place of service is."

That He is there, in that eternal sanctuary by virtue of His "once for all" sacrifice, which consecrates Him for evermore, is hinted at in verse 3, but more fully developed in Chapter ix. The sphere of His priestly ministry is emphatically stated in verse 4, the *type* being Aaron, but the *order* Melchisedec. The use of the present tense in verse 4 proves that the temple was standing when this letter was written. What a solemn revelation is this, that those priests in the temple in Jerusalem were busily serving not a *living* God, but a *dead* ritual in a *rejected temple*, from which God and His glory had withdrawn.

In verse 2, He is called the "public minister" of this *sanctuary* and *tabernacle*, which is called in Chapter ix. 11, "a greater and more perfect tabernacle." It is the divine original of which the tabernacle in the wilderness was but a copy.

In this *eternal* sanctuary there is officiating an *eternal* priest, one in His own eternal being, possessing true manhood and indissoluble life, and presenting in all its abiding efficacy a sacrifice which was offered through an *eternal* spirit. Everything is stamped with *eternity*. His ministry is a more excellent ministry. His mediation is that of a *better* covenant of which He is the "*covenant victim*." Thus we have type contrasted with antitype, shadow with substance, old covenant with new, that which is purely symbolical with the real and eternal. We have the priesthood, ministry, tabernacle, mediation contrasted, and we behold *Christ Superior and Supreme*.

The Chapter ends with the covenants contrasted. Of the old it is said it was not faultless (verse 7). "It decayeth and waxeth old, ready to vanish away" (verse 13). The priesthood, sacrifice and ritual of the old covenant perfected nothing. Its fulfilment depended on the faithfulness of a people concerning whom God said "They *continued* not in my covenant, and I *regarded them* not saith the Lord" (verse 9). There disobedience wrecked everything. It had no *covenant victim*, the blood of which could cleanse, and the priest of which was able to bring them as "*perfected worshippers*" within the vail. This covenant not only bound them to perfect obedience, but it committed God to punish every act of disobedience. It was "this do and thou shalt live" to a people who *could not* do. It was written on stone, and was as cold and dead as the stone on which it was written, in the impartation of either obedience or life.

The *better covenant* had the blood of a divine sacrifice, an *intelligent* and *willing* victim. Chapter

vii. 22 presents Him as its *surety*, and Chapter **viii.** 6 brings Him before us as its *mediator*.

It is not a bridge resting on pillars (like the *old covenant*) that were divine and human, but it is a bridge resting on pillars *altogether* divine, founded on His own blood and mediated by our risen and eternal Lord.

Note it in no way depends on the creatures' obedience, but on the faithfulness of the creator (*e.g.*, verses 10, 11) :—

    " I will make a new covenant.
    I will put, etc.
    I will write, etc.
    I will be to them for a God.
    I will be merciful.
    I will remember no more their sins.
    I will remember no more their iniquities.

And

    They shall be to me a people.
    They shall not teach every man his neighbour.
    They shall not teach every man his brother.
    For *all* shall know Me."

This assures its abiding and eternal characteristics in the experience of those who are *in it*.

More than once I have asked the reader to note that this letter is to " Hebrews." Here again it is distinctly stated, " Behold the days come, saith the Lord, when I will make a new covenant with the *House of Israel*, and with the *House of Judah* " (verse 8). We have not only forestalled them in these covenant blessings, " They are enemies for our sakes " (Rom. xi. 28) ; but we are what they are not, we are in the *Covenanter Himself*. So this Chapter brings before us a sanctuary, real and genuine, whose builder and maker is God, the heavenly and eternal, which Moses saw in the Mount, when he was admonished by God, " see thou make everything according to the pattern " (Ex. xxv. 9), therefor, its high priest must of necessity be greater than Aaron. He must not only be human, but also Divine. He must be more than *typically* and *ceremonially* holy. He must be actually and intrinsically holy. He must possess a sacrifice to offer, the blood of which must be eternally efficacious, and He Himself must be that *covenant victim*. The covenant of which He is both surety and mediator must be one worthy of God, a sanctuary heavenly and eternal, God in manhood, its eternal priest, and also its eternal sacrifice. The *covenant victim*, securing for all the covenant people, *eternally* the full atoning value of His death, and not only procuring it thus for them, but also producing in them the everlasting acceptance, perfection and full knowledge of all He died to secure.

ANALYSIS OF CHAPTER

THE CROWN-ALL. KEYNOTE. " A more excellent ministry " (v. 6).

CONTENTS.

1. Priesthood.
2. Tabernacle.
3. Covenant.

PRIESTHOOD.

1. Order. Melchisedec (chap. vii.).
2. Pattern. Aaron.
3. A Ministering Priest (v. 2).
4. In the Heavenly Sanctuary (v. 2).

CONTRASTS.

1. Christ and Aaron.
2. Old and New Tabernacle.
3. Old and New Covenant.
4. Worship : Past and Present.
5. Place of Worship : Past and Present.

ESSENTIALS OF WORSHIP. *Past.*

1. A Sanctuary.
2. A Priest and Minister.
3. A Sacrifice.

ESSENTIALS OF WORSHIP. *To-day.*

1. A Sanctuary (Holy of Holies).
2. A True Tabernacle.
3. God-made and Eternal.
4. A Great High Priest its Minister, who must be
5. Inherently and Eternally Holy.
6. Himself Man.
7. His Priesthood must be associated with
8. The Heavenly Sanctuary, and He
9. An Eternal Priest.
10. He must have something to offer, and that must be
11. A Sacrifice Eternally Abiding in its Efficacy.

ALL THIS WE HAVE.

1. The Sanctuary and True Tabernacle (v. 2).
2. Greater and more Perfect Tabernacle (chap. ix. 11).
3. Not made with hands (chap. ix. 24).
4. Such an High Priest and Minister (v. 2).
5. Royal (after the order of Melchisedec) (chap. v. 10).
6. Set on the right hand of the Majesty
7. In the Heavens (v. 1).
8. Prophetic Word. " Sit Thou," " Thou art " (Psa. cx. 1-4).

9. A Ministering Priest with something to offer (v. 3).
10. His own Sacrifice of Himself (chap. vii. 27).
11. Final. Complete, Eternal (chap. x. 12).

> *Note.—Not a Priest on earth* (chap. viii. 4). A Heavenly and Eternal Priest, offering His "once-for-all" sacrifice inside the veil of a Divine, Heavenly and Eternal Tabernacle.

THE NEW AND BETTER COVENANT. Having

A Divine Surety (chap. vii. 22).
A Divine Mediator (chap. viii. 7).

THE OLD COVENANT.

1. Faulty.
2. They continued not in it.
3. I regarded them not.
4. External (on stone).
5. Could not remove sin (chap. x. 4).
6. Could not bring men to God (chap. ix.; comp. chap. vii. 19).
7. Waxed old (v. 13).
8. Vanished away (v. 13).
9. Its Priesthood and Law changed (chap. vii. 12).

NEW COVENANT.

1. Prophetically foretold (Jer. xxxi. 31-34).
2. Historically fulfilled (Luke xxii. 20).
3. My Laws into their minds. Perfect knowledge of it.
4. Write them upon their hearts. Perfect obedience to it.
5. An Everlasting Covenant (Heb. xiii. 20).
6. Its sacrifice eternally efficacious (v. 12).
7. Its Priest constituted by an everlasting oath (chap. vii. 22).

8. God to them for a God.
9. They to Him for a people.
10. Free access . . . It brings to God (chaps. vii.
   18 ; x. 19-22).
11. Worshippers eternally and consciously purged
   (chap. x. 2, 14).
12. Its Surety and Mediator—" Jesus " (chaps.
   vii. 29 ; viii. 6).

> " Thy Cross alone, O Christ,
> Could bear the awful load
> Which none in heaven nor earth
> Could bear, but God."

The measure of His acceptance is the measure
of ours. The something which He has to offer
which fills His priestly hands is the very same thing
which must fill ours, and the sphere of His priestly
ministry, viz., " The Heavenly Sanctuary and the
Tabernacle " must be the sphere of our priestly
worship. We are a *Heavenly* priesthood which
must worship within the vail.

List of words used in this Chapter, and nowhere
else found in the New Testament :—

1. **επηξεν**— epexen (v. 2), translated " pitched."
   This verb is used by The Septuagint in
   Isaiah xlii. 5.

2. **νενομοθετηται**—nenomothetētai (v. 6), translated " was established." This word is also
   used in chap. vii. 11.

3. **αφανισμος**—aphanismos (v. 13), translated
   " vanish away." This word is found in The
   Septuagint, so also No. 2.

CHAPTER IX

CHRIST—GREATER THAN THE TABERNACLE, ITS VESSELS AND RITUAL

IN Chapter VIII we had the two covenants contrasted, here, in this Chapter, we have a detail of the holy vessels of administration, including sanctuary, furnishings, priesthood and sacrifices ending in the necessity and value of Christ's once-for-all offering. His entrance into and work in the sanctuary and true tabernacle with His second advent. The Chapter opens with the statement that the first sanctuary had its ordinances of divine service, and a *worldly* sanctuary with its vessels of divine service. The reference to these is only a passing one for it is said, "Concerning which we cannot now speak particularly," or as it is in margin "in detail." In the description of the "Holiest," the golden censer is seen within the veil. This is a most important statement, for it was only on the great day of atonement that it was there, taken in by the high priest (*see* Lev. xvi. 12, 13). This statement gives us the key to the chapter. It must be read and interpreted as the great antitype of what took place in the tabernacle on that day, when the high priest alone entered through the veil, and that not without blood. Concerning this we read, "The Holy Spirit this signifying that the way into the Holiest was not yet made manifest, while as the first tabernacle was yet standing, which was a figure for the time Now present" (verses 8, 9). Note no free access for priest or people, way not manifested, no sacrifices efficacious enough to rend the veil, and give free access. The revisers have made a very important alteration in verse 9. Instead of "Time *then* present," they render it Time *now* present, *i.e.*, God's parables for this present time. How important then is the study of the tabernacle *read* and *interpreted* in the light of this wonderful epistle. Might not one say that the abounding confusion and darkness to-day among so many of God's people *re* the great question of *worship*, as to *how*, *when* and *where* is directly traceable to their ignorance of these types.

In contrast to all Levitical ritual is the more excellent ministry of Christ. He entered as our great high priest into the *true, greater* and *more perfect* tabernacle, *i.e.*, into heaven itself (verse 24), and entered by His own blood. In this wonderful chapter blood occurs *twelve* times, emphasising its full administrative value, as seen, known, and valued by God. When Aaron entered once a year, he obtained an annual redemption (and then *only* in *figure*), *i.e.*, till the next day of atonement, when a fresh entering, with a fresh sacrifice was essential. The great contrast to this appears in verse 11, where Christ is seen entering by a more excellent tabernacle, with (in the sense of, BY) His own blood, having obtained *eternal redemption*. In this verse note margin, Good things *that have* come. When Aaron entered, he passed through the gate by the altar and later through the first and second veil into the immediate presence of God. He passed through the tabernacle into the tabernacle. We read, " But Christ having become an high priest of good things that *have* come by (or through) a greater and more perfect tabernacle not made with hands," etc. The question is

what is this *greater* and *more* perfect tabernacle
through which He has become an high priest of
good things that have come ? Many have difficulties here, and these are caused by connecting the
more perfect tabernacle with His entering instead
of with His priesthood. I suggest the apostle
connects it with His priesthood. If this be right,
that would emphasise *the true humanity* of Christ
in resurrection entering upon His everlasting
priesthood. " This day have I begotten Thee,
Thou art a priest for ever " (Heb. v. 6).

In verses 13-14, we have the great difference
between the blood of beasts slain unwillingly
and without knowledge, and the blood of Christ,
who through the eternal spirit offered Himself
without spot to God, a *willing, intelligent* and
devoted sacrifice, animated in His offering by an
eternal spirit. Here I would more definitely state,
than I do in the analysis attached, my belief that
Eternal Spirit here, although without the article,
means the Holy Spirit of God. There is an in-
creasing tendency among some teachers, to refuse
to accept, as meaning the third person of the
Trinity, certain passages in which holy spirit and
spirit occur without the article, such, as Rom. i. 4,
" spirit of holiness " ; and 1 Peter iii. 18,
" quickened in spirit." Now in *both* these passages
I believe it is the blessed spirit of God that is
meant and *not* Christ's own spirit. Himself, in
verse 14, is emphatic the great key word of the
Epistle, the incomparable One. God's superlative
Christ.

In verse 15, His sacrifice is seen to be retrospective, as well as present and prospective,
covering all time. The eternal spirit lifts the
sacrifice above all limitations of time and space.
It must be so, for it is impossible for the blood

of bulls and goats to take away sins (Heb. x. 4) ;
hence they all awaited His death. It is the
eternal sacrifice of an eternal priest, in an eternal
sanctuary. He is the Lamb slain from the
foundation of the world.

Under the first covenant God bestows on Israel
an inheritance which was to be theirs conditionally.
These conditions they so failed to keep, and so
burdened the inheritance, that the testator Himself must die, and redeem the inheritance, so that
the people might obtain the promise of Eternal
inheritance.

The Chapter from verse 24 closes with the
present mediation of Christ in holy places of the
Eternal and heavenly sanctuary, of which the
tabernacle was but a copy, His being manifested
in the presence of God for us, His present manifestation, but it also goes on to speak of His future
manifestation " sin apart " unto salvation. " They
that wait for Him," has a distinct reference to the
millions of Israel on the great day of atonement,
waiting for the appearance of Aaron at the end
of the busy day of atonement, appearing in his
robes of glory and beauty, apart from sin, unto
salvation (Lev. xvi. 23, 24). Please note that you
cannot base on " *They that wait for Him,*" the
" partial rapture " theory, *i.e.*, " Only those who
are waiting." The type helps us here. Aaron
came out in glory and blessing to all and for all,
for whom he had taken in the blood. He took it
in for *all Israel*, so he came out for *all Israel*. So
here in Heb. 9, Christ will be manifested to all in
the covenant, and for whom He went in with His
own *covenant* blood.

Whom He justified, *them* He also glorified (Rom.
viii. 30), justified by sovereign grace, and glorified
by the same grace.

Please note the second advent, and " The Lord's Coming," are two distinct truths. His second advent is His Mount Olivet Descent (Zech. xiv). His coming as King to reign, His manifestation in glory, when every eye shall see Him. The coming of our Lord, as we read it in the Epistles, is His coming in the clouds of heaven for " His Church," when she shall meet him in the air and be with Him and like Him for ever in *heavenly glory*. The Old Testament Scriptures are full of His advent, but contain not one single reference to His coming into the clouds for His church. His church is a secret, hid from the most favoured recipients of His will in the past dispensations. So also His coming for her must of necessity be so.

ANALYSIS OF CHAPTER

CONTENTS.

1. Melchisedec and Aaron.
2. Their Sanctuaries.
3. Their Sacrifices.
4. Their Covenants.

TYPE (Leviticus xvi.).—The great Day of Atonement. This is seen in the fact of the censer being within the veil (v. 4) and in the reappearing in benediction of the priest (v. 28).

MELCHISEDEC AND AARON CONTRASTED.

1. In their ministries.
2. In their offerings.
3. In their sanctuaries.
4. In their results.

F

AARON MINISTERED.

1. In a worldly sanctuary (v. 1).
2. Into which he entered once yearly (v. 7)
3. With blood of creature victims (v. 7) ;
4. Shed for himself and the people (v. 7) ;
5. Which could not take away sins (chap. x. 4) ;
6. Which could not give free access (chap. ix. 8);
7. Which could not perfect the conscience (chap. ix. 14) ;
8. Which was offered yearly (chap. x. 1).

MELCHISEDEC MINISTERS

1. In the Sanctuary and true Tabernacle (v. 11 ; chap. viii. 2) ;
2. Into which He once for all entered (v. 12) ;
3. Through His own blood
4. Shed for others, not for Himself,
5. Which took away sins (v. 28) ;
6. Which gave boldness for the access ;
7. Which perfected the worshipper's conscience (v. 14) ;
8. Which was offered once for all.

> *Note.*—The presence or absence of a worldly Sanctuary determines the character of a *Dispensation* as to whether it is earthly or Heavenly. The Patriarchal Dispensation lasted 2500 years. It had no worldly Sanctuary, hence it was a Heavenly Dispensation, and those Patriarchs were a Heavenly people—strangers and pilgrims in the earth who sought a city which had foundations whose builder and maker is God.

THE WORLDLY SANCTUARIES.

1. The Tabernacle, lasting 500 years.
2. The Temple, lasting 400 years.
3. Zerubbabel's Temple, lasting 500 years.
4. Herod's Temple, lasting 89½ years.
5. The Temple in which Antichrist sits.
6. Ezekiel's Millennial Temple.

> *Note.*—These are the only worldly Sanctuaries mentioned in the Scriptures. This Dispensation has no

worldly Sanctuary. Hence it is a Heavenly Dispensation. Those saved in it are a Heavenly people who worship in the True and Eternal Tabernacle, within the veil. It is of immense importance to see this great truth, for any place of worship to-day, whether it be cathedral, abbey, church, chapel or building, is a denial of the true and Heavenly, and their ministering priests a denial of Him who is the High Priest and Minister of the Heavenly Sanctuary " which the Lord has pitched and not man " (Heb. viii. 1, 2) ; God's saints to-day are His priests, and they worship within the veil.

God's first dwelling-place among His people was a Tabernacle, then a Temple, then a Church ; again a Temple, and finally and eternally a Tabernacle (Rev. xxi. 3).

THE SACRIFICES CONTRASTED.

I. *Aaron's.*

1. Atonement only typical.
2. Blood of goats and bulls.
3. Ashes of an heifer.
4. Unwilling and unconscious victims.
5. Whose blood could not
6. Purge the conscience from dead works
7. To serve the Living God ;
8. Hence could not give free access.
9. Could only redeem in type,
10. And that only for a year (chap. x. 3).

II. *Christ's.*

1. Atonement actual.
2. The sacrifice of His own blood
3. Shed once for all.
4. The great substance and antitype
5. Purges the conscience,
6. Removes moral guilt,
7. Opens a way into the Holiest,
8. Brings the worshipper purged to God (chap. x. 2, 19),

9. Redeems actually (v. 12),
10. Redeems Eternally (v. 12).

> *Note.—A Holy and Eternal Priest offering a Holy and Eternal Sacrifice through an Eternal Spirit in a Heavenly and Eternal Sanctuary.*
>
> Through an Eternal Spirit (v. 14), I understand for various reasons to be the Holy Spirit of God, but it is only right to say that some scholarly and godly expositors hold and teach that it is not *the Holy Spirit*, but His own Spirit showing forth His eternal attitude to His Father in the plan of redemption. The Lamb slain from the foundation of the world (Rev. xiii. 8). The One who was verily foreordained before the foundation of the world (1 Peter i. 20).

THE TWO COVENANTS.—*The First and Old* (Heb. viii. 13).

1. A death essential of
2. The Covenant victim.
3. Blood of calves and goats.
4. Sprinkling the Covenant,
5. Sprinkling the Tabernacle,
6. Sprinkling the people,
7. Thus binding God and people ;
8. They to perfect obedience,
9. God to judgment of disobedience.

The New Covenant.

1. Death essential (v. 16).
2. This death, that of the Covenanter.
3. He the Son of God.
4. His death retrospective and prospective.
5. For the redemption of transgressions
6. Under both Covenants.
7. To obtain the Eternal Inheritance
8. For the called of both Covenants.
9. To make the Covenant valid (v. 17).
10. Purge once for all the people.
11. Purify the real and Heavenly Tabernacle,
12. The true Holies of which the first was a Type.

THE SON ITS MEDIATOR (v. 15). Even He who was its Testator, is its Mediator, because of His perfect effectual and final sacrifice.

> *Note.*—Christ as the Mediator is so qualified for this work because He died a death that purged His people once and for ever from their sins. A death that settled for ever the sin and sins question, *i.e.* what they were and what they did. A sacrifice efficacious enough to purge once and for ever the people, the Covenant and its true Sanctuary, to which He has gone to make eternally good on their behalf, the every thing He secured for them on the Cross. Every offering in the Old Covenant that was taken into the holies had died without, so Christ goes in by virtue of His death without. What a Mediator! So intensely interested in both (God and His people), in the nature of both " The God Man," so our true " Day's Man " (Job ix. 33).

HE ENTERS (verses 24-28).

1. The Holiest above,
2. Of which the Tabernacle was a copy.
3. To be manifested for us
4. Before God.
5. To offer Himself there
6. In the finality of His sacrifice,
7. Not often as of old,
8. But once for all,
9. Having put away sin and sins (vv. 26, 28).

MAN'S APPOINTMENT.

Death. " Once to die."

CHRIST'S APPOINTMENT.

Death. " So Christ was once offered."
Sacrificial. " To bear the sins of many."

MAN'S APPOINTMENT.

Judgment. " After this, Judgment."

CHRIST'S APPOINTMENT.

He shall appear (be seen)
By a waiting people
A second time
Apart from sin
Unto salvation.

Note.—Some attempt to teach from this passage what is known as "*The Partial Rapture,*" *i.e.* only the looking ones are taken. This is a very SERIOUS ERROR which no one rightly dividing the Word of truth can hold. This Scripture in no way suggests such a thought. The Revisers translate "them that *wait* for Him." The type we have seen is

THE GREAT DAY OF ATONEMENT (Lev. 16).
The order of which was—

1. Two goats taken.
2. Lots cast to determine the sacrificial goat.
3. It was slain and blood taken in.
4. Aaron came out to a people
5. With all their sins and transgressions
6. Unconfessed and upon them ;
7. Confessed same on head of
8. Live goat (scapegoat)
9. Which took them all away.
10. Aaron again goes in,
11. Removes his sacrificial robes ;
12. Comes out in robes of glory and beauty
13. To bless in Jehovah's Name
14. The waiting millions of Israel.

Note.—He came out to all those for whom He took *in the blood.* Not for a few, *but for all.* Such is the teaching of the great antitype (Heb. ix). He is coming in priestly benediction to all those for whom He went in. He died for all, He is the Mediator of all. He comes for all for whom He went in.

The atoning work is done,
The Victim's blood is shed ;
And Jesus now is gone
His people's cause to plead.

He stands in Heaven their great High Priest,
And bears their names upon His breast.
And though awhile He be
Hid from the eyes of men,
His people look to see
Their great High Priest again.
In brightest glory He will come
And take His *waiting* people home.

Words found in this chapter, and found nowhere else in the New Testament :—

1. **Θυματηριον**—thumaterion (v. 4), translated " Censer." Much has been written of old time, which is said to make this word mean either " the censer " or altar of incense. The revisers have in their margin "or altar of incense." That the censer is the true translation here is beyond all dispute, for it is seen with in the veil, in " the holiest of all." In this the golden altar never was. The censer was only there on the Great Day of Atonement. This fact gives the key to all the chapter, and stamps it as the great substance of Leviticus xvi. " The great day of atonement."

2. **Σταμνος**—stamnos (v. 4), translated " pot."

3. **Κατασκία ζονται**—kataskiazontai (v. 5), translated " shadowing."

4. **αγνωηματων.**—agnōēmatōn (v. 7), translated " errors." Revisers in margin give *Gk.* ignorances, *i.e.*, " sins of ignorance."

5. **δίκαίωμασίν**—dikaiōmasin (v. 10), translated " ordinances."

6. **δαμαλεως**—damaliōs (v. 13), translated " Heifer." Here is a direct reference to the sacrifice of the red heifer in Numbers xix.

7. **Τραγων**—tragōn (vv. 12, 13, 19), translated "goats." This word is also found in chap. x. 4.

8. **εγκεκαίνισται**—egkekainistai (v. 18), translated "was dedicated." This word is also found in chap. x. 20.

9. **αἱματεκχυσίας**—haimatekkusias (v. 22), translated "shedding of blood."

Words Nos. 1, 2, 4, 6, 7, 8 are found in The Septuagint.

CHAPTER X

CHRIST—GREATER THAN THE SACRIFICES

IN the first eighteen verses of this chapter we have the sum of what we have already been considering. It opens with the declaration that the law is the shadow of good things that are coming, not the very image, but the shadow. We have already been occupied with some of these great shadows, and we have seen them fulfilled in Christ. You never can have a shadow without a substance and our blessed Lord is the great substance which down through the ages has cast His shadow. Therefore, God is ever so jealous of His types, for you cannot alter a shadow one hair's-breadth without changing the substance, and the substance is Christ. These shadows were not able to perfect or purge the worshipper. This is seen in the necessity of fresh victims and fresh blood shedding *year by year*. The reason of this is given by God, " For it is impossible for the blood of bulls and goats to take away sins," so, *annually*, there was a *remembrance* of sins. We thus see a very striking difference between the standing of the *Old* Testament worshipper and the *New*. The difference is not so much a question of faith as it is the *blood* of a victim. The whole Levitical economy did not and could not provide such a *victim*. It only typified *the coming* one.

In verse 5, we have this coming one introduced, foretold in Psalm xl, 6-8. These words of the psalmist are thus transferred to Christ, and the Jews accepted them as such.

In verse 6, the apostle takes the reading of The Septuagint, "A body has thou prepared me." He of whom this psalm speaks is truly the man of "*the digged ear*," God's perfect servant (*see* Ex. xxi. 1-6; Deut. xv. 12-17; Isaiah, xlviii, 8; l. 5). "Thou has taught me to hear and obey," so that it is not sacrifice, but obedience in which God delights. "A body has thou prepared me" emphasises the descent of Philippians ii., from heights which no finite mind can scale to depths, which no finite mind can ever fathom, the *slave* form, the *man* likeness, the *perfect* obedience, even unto death, of the Son of God.

"In the volume of the book," verse 7, refers to the Old Testament scriptures, if, indeed, it does not refer to the purpose of God in the counsels of eternity, the marking out of the path, as "like God," which this blessed one should tread, accepting the Father's will for Him, and in every detail giving effect to it, even unto the death of the Cross. The law prophets and Psalms (Luke xxiv. 26-27) were possessed, loved, read, studied, understood and obeyed by our great Saviour.

The one great grand and supreme act of obedience was *Calvary*, this is very clearly stated in verse 10. We see Him here as the great antitype of all those Levitical sacrifices in which we see Him foretold and foreslain.

There are three great words in this chapter: "*purged for ever* (verse 2), "*Sanctified for ever*" (verse 10), "*perfected for ever*" (verse 14), and this as worshippers. This we have in type in the sanctification and consecration of the Aaronic priesthood in Leviticus viii. not forgetting to notice that remarkable passage, "And they shall eat those things of which the atonement was made, to *consecrate* and to *sanctify* them " (Exod. xxix. 33). In the Hebrew tongue to consecrate a priest is to fill his hands, in the Greek tongue it is to " *perfect him.*"

We have, then, the perfect, complete, and eternal Purging, Sanctifying and Perfecting by the once for all sacrifice of Calvary, the priestly house of our Great High Priest.

This is emphasised thus, " And every priest *standeth* daily ministering and offering the same sacrifices which can never take away sins. But this man, after he had offered one sacrifice for sins for ever, sat down on the right hand of God " (verses 11, 12). The doctrinal part of this letter closes at verse 18, having brought before us the supremacy and sufficiency of our Great High Priest in all His *personal, official* and *moral* glories, and above all magnifying His great sacrifice.

> " In the Cross of Christ I glory,
> Towering o'er the wreck of time,
> All the light of sacred story
> Gathers round its head sublime."

From verse 19 to end we begin a new section which assures us that because of His obedience in death God has highly exalted Him, and that through His death and resurrection " *the way* " into the holiest has been made manifest (compare Chapter ix. 8). The gospel of free access is proclaimed, and the command is, " Let us draw nigh." His blood imparts the confidence for the entrance. The word translated, " new," is only found here in the New Testament scriptures and means newly slain, blood that is never cold or coagulated, a death that is *ever present*, a cross that is but yesterday. Here we learn that Christ incarnate is the great antitype of the veil. The veil which in type so effectually shut God in from His people, and His people out from Him, has its substance in the humanity of our Lord. If it were simply the life of the Lord we had for our salvation, then we, of all men, would be most miserable and hopeless, for His holy life would *the more condemn* us and the more effectually *shut us* out. But the veil was rent (Matt. xxvii. 51). The blow of judgment which slew the Lamb rent the veil and thus the way into the holiest—yea, into the innermost shrine of God's abiding and unsullied holiness—was opened up whereby men who *are* sinners can draw nigh and stand acceptably there.

> " Accepted I am in the once offered Lamb,
> 'Twas God who Himself had devised the plan."

" Having a great priest over the House of God." This term " the House of God " surely includes, in the exercise of His priesthood, all saved ones, and as to its sphere, surely it is " the sanctuary and true tabernacle which the Lord pitched, and not man " (Heb. viii. 2). Those who by their belief and teaching would limit this " priestly work and House " to any section of the professing Church on earth, not only *dishonour the* priest, but *belittle* and *beggar* His great work, and become themselves utterly deceived.

The remainder of the chapter is devoted to a most solemn warning as to the terrible position of an " *apostate*." It is a parallel passage to Chapter vi. The word " wilfully " points to deliberate and high-handed rebellion. It does not refer *to an* act, but *a course* (*see* Num. xv. 30 ; Ps. xix. 12, 13 ; and Heb. vi. 4-6 ; 2 Pet. ii. 20-22). Here in Hebrews it is in keeping with

the character of the whole epistle, and refers to
an apostate, one who renounces the Christ and
goes back to Judaism and becomes an adversary.
The writer is not stating a particular case, but
assuming one, for he closes his exhortation with
these words, " But we are not of them who draw
back into perdition, but of them who believe
unto the salvation of the soul." His great longing
and care for them is seen in his " Cast not away
therefore your confidence which has great recom-
pence of reward," lest in a weak moment under
the awful stress and strain of terrible persecutions
they might falter and renounce Christ. To
appreciate this we really need to be a Hebrew,
a Hebrew not only in the day of the epistle's first
going forth, but a Hebrew to-day, whose confession of Christ costs him everything that the
heart of man counts dear.

ANALYSIS OF CHAPTER.

CONTENTS.

1. The shadow and substance contrasted (vv.
   1-10).
2. The worshippers contrasted (vv. 2, 19, 20).
3. The Priesthood contrasted (v. 11).
4. Exhortations based thereon (vv. 32-39).
5. Price of Faith   ,,
6. Need of Endurance   ,,
7. Reward and Loss   ,,

OLD COVENANT AND SINS.

1. Sacrifices ineffectual.
2. Could not take away sins (vv. 4, 11).
3. " Bulls and Goats " (Lev. xvi ; Day of
   Atonement).

4. Remembrance of sins ; yearly (v. 3).
5. Worshipper never purged (v. 2).
6. Gave God no pleasure (v. 6).
7. Its priesthood a drudgery (v. 11).

NEW COVENANT.

1. Victim. Eternal. Intelligent.
2. Sacrifice. Voluntary.
3. In God's will and pleasure (v. 7).
4. Forewritten and ordained (v. 7).
5. Accomplishing the will of God (v. 8).
6. Fulfilling every shadow (v. 9).
7. Removing the old (v. 9).
8. Establishing a perfect and eternal Atonement.
9. Purging for ever. The worshippers.
10. Sanctifying. The worshippers (v. 10).
11. Perfecting for ever the worshippers (v. 14).
12. Removed a sacrificing priesthood (v. 11).
13. With its *standing* drudgery.
14. Bringing a priesthood of rest (seated).
15. By an eternal sacrifice.

> *Note.*—We have three great words used in connection with the worshippers. " Purged," *i.e.* Cleansed. " Sanctified," *i.e.* Separated to God. " Perfected," *i.e.* To completely place unto perpetuity in a *finished fitness*, the worshipper, the covenant relationship, and fellowship being secured not simply for a year, but for ever.

> " We thank Thee for the precious blood,
>   The blood by which our souls draw nigh
> All cleansed and sanctified to God,
>   Thy holy Name to magnify."

ESSENTIALS OF WORSHIP.

1. The place (v. 19).
2. The priest (v. 21).
3. The sacrifice (v. 12).

THE HEAVENS IN HEBREWS.

1. Material (chaps. i. 10 ; xi. 12 ; xii. 26).
2. His pathway (chap. iv. 14 ; passed through).
3. He enters (chap. ix. 24).
4. Sits down (chaps. viii. 1 ; i. 3 ; x. 12).
5. He made higher (chap. vii. 26).

> *Note.—Heaven itself* (ix. 24), I take to be the great original of " The Sanctuary " in the wilderness, the innermost shrine of God's abiding presence, the place where we " *draw nigh*."

BOLDNESS FOR OUR ENTRANCE SECURED.

1. By the Blood of Jesus (v. 19).
2. By a New (*i.e.* newly slain ; v. 20).
3. And Living Way.
4. Through the Veil.
5. God incarnate, *crucified*.
6. Having a Great Priest (v. 21).
7. House of God (*i.e.* The Sanctuary and True Tabernacle. The place where He is minister).
8. Divine beseechment (v. 22). Let us draw Near etc.

MORAL FITNESS OF WORSHIPPERS SECURED.

1. A true heart (*see* chaps. iv. 12 ; viii. 10 ; x. 16).
2. Fullness of faith.
3. Hearts sprinkled from an evil conscience (chaps. x. 2 ; ix. 14).
4. Body washed with pure water (Exod. xxix ; Lev. viii).

> *Note.*—" Hearts sprinkled " and " Body washed " throw us back on the types, viz. : The Sanctification and Consecration of the Priestly House (Ex. xxix ; Lev. viii) ; also, the Sacrifice of the Red Heifer in Numbers xix, for our enlightenment of these two statements.

EXHORTATIONS (vv. 23-31).

1. Hold fast our confession.
2. Without waverings.
3. Consider one another.
4. Provoke to love and good works.
5. Not forsaking the Assemblings.
6. Of ourselves together.
7. Avoid wilful sinning (*Note*, not an act, but a state ; *see* verb).
8. No sacrifice for such a state.
9. The old Covenant possessed none.
10. Wilful sin was unto death (1 John v. 16).
11. The Lord will judge *His people* (Deut. xxxii. 10-43).

REMEMBER (vv. 32-34).

1. Former days when you
2. Were *illuminated* (*i.e.* saved).
3. Ye endured a great fight.
4. Were a gazing stock.
5. Reproached, afflicted.
6. Lost your earthly all.
7. Fact of heavenly and enduring substance.

> *Note.*—Surely these were the days of their first love, the days of the kindness of their youth. Days of which we, too, need to be reminded.

EXHORTATION (vv. 35-39).

1. Cast not away your confidence.
2. Which hath great recompense of reward (2 John viii).
3. Have patience, do God's will, receive the reward.
4. The Lord is quickly Coming.
5. Draw not back to loss (Gal. ii. 12) (*i.e.* to Judaism).

6. Keep believing to the
7. Preservation of the soul.

Note.—This exhortation does not raise the question of their eternal salvation from wrath to life eternal, but it does raise the question of rewards, a most solemn and neglected truth for these days.

Words found in this chapter, and nowhere else in the New Testament :—

1. **διηνεκες**—Diēnekes (vv. 1, 12, 14), translated "continually" In verses 12 and 14 it is translated "for ever." This word is also found in chapter vii. 3.

2. **Τηαγων**—Tēagōn (v. 4), translated "Goats." This word is also used in chap. ix. 12, 13, 19.

3. **Ενεκαίνισεν**—Enekainisen (v. 20), translated "consecrated." This word is also found in chap. ix. 18 ; where it is translated "dedicated."

4. **αχλινη**—aklinē (v. 23), translated "without wavering."

5. **Προσφατων**—prosphatōn (v. 20), translated "New." This word is "New" in the sense of "newly slain" Calvary is only yesterday. The blood which gives us boldness for the entrance is fresh and warm, never cold or coagulated. It is living for our Lord in resurrection is Himself "the way."

6. **Φοβερα**—Phobera (vv. 27, 31), translated "fearful." This word is also used in chap. xii. 1.

7. **Εκδοχη**—ekdoxē (v. 27), "looking for."

8. **Τιμωριας**—timōrias (v. 29), translated "punishment."

G

9. **Ενυβρισας**—enubrisas (v. 29), translated "despite." The word means "*insult*."

10. **Αθλησιν**—athlēsin (v. 32), translated "fright."

11. **Θεατρίζομενοί**—theatrizomenoi (v. 33), translated "gazing stock." Our English word theatre comes from this word.

12. **συνεπαθησατε**—sunepathēsate (v. 39), translated "draw back."

13. **ὑποστολης**—hupostolēs (v. 34), translated "compassion." Used also chap. iv. 15.

Words Nos. 1, 2, 3, 5, 6, 9 are found in The Septuagint.

CHAPTER XI

FAITH'S TYPES, HEROES AND VICTORIES

HEBREWS xi

THE analysis of this Chapter being so full, I must somewhat curtail its summary. Surely it is a wonderful picture-gallery of God's great dead! In throwing them on the canvas God confines Himself to their faith—not their failures but their triumphs—reminding us of the words " Then shall every man have praise of God " 1 Cor. iv. 5. The chapter is linked up in a definite way with the 39th verse of chapter x. " But of them which believe unto the salvation of their souls." It brings before us the meaning of believing, and then gives us to see faith in action, in the life of the one who possesses it, shewing us first what it is (vv. 1-3), and then what it does.

Faith is not a dispensation word like " Church," " Body," " Mystery," " Bride," " New Man," " In Christ," but is a word which had a tremendous force in all dispensations, and apart from which it is impossible to please God, expressing as it does the relationship and experiences of God's elect in all time. We read " Faith without works is dead," hence this chapter, the great classic of faith, is full of works. In its opening it presents to us in a very remarkable way, the Typical Men of Genesis, and also in their typical order, beginning with " Abel." He is a type of that faith which believes God as to his ruin and lays hold of the sacrifice as God's own providing to meet

99

D

that ruin, an Abel death, for he died in his lamb, and an Abel resurrection, for he rose in his lamb. This brings us to the experience of every true believer. We died with Christ. " For ye died and your life is hid with Christ in God " (Col. iii. 3). Then we have " *Enoch*," the habit of whose life was to walk with God. An Enoch walk in the power of an Abel death. Even so, we also should walk in newness of life (Rom. vi. 4). Enoch is a very wonderful picture of " the Church," for he was raptured ere the flood came, thus saved *from* it as Noah was saved through it. So, ere the great tribulation will have come, the Church of the Dispensation will be " caught up," translated, for God has not appointed *us* to wrath (1 Thess. v. 9).

Enoch's habitual walk with God emphasises the great fact that holiness of life is inseparable from faith in the dying Lamb of Calvary.

Noah, a preacher of righteousness, illustrates the saved remnant of Israel in a coming day and other saved ones with them (Rev. vii), brought safely through the judgment and wrath and persecutions of the " great tribulation." Note Noah's testimony was in the power of an Enoch walk.

Abraham, the great central figure of faith, not so much the faith that saves, as the faith that believes God all the way. Faith in resurrection, believing that out of a *dead* body and womb God could and would bring life, that God Himself was the quickener. This faith produced Isaac. The faith that hopeth all things, believeth all things that cries :—

> " I would rather walk in the dark with God
> Than go alone in the light."

Isaac illustrates the great truth of sonship. Note his miraculous conception, his circumcision, feeding, weaning, mocking and his triumph over his enemies (Gen. xxi) ; then in Chapter xxii his whole burnt-offering on the mountain in Moriah's land. He and the ram being typical of God's only-begotten Son on that same mount two thousand years after, literally offered up for Abram and his seed (Heb. ii. 16). Jacob illustrates the truest and highest service, the *service of " sonship."* We see him the heir of all an outcast in a far-off country, serving in order to bring back with him to the everlasting inheritance, the bride of his love and choice, picture of Him of whom we sing :—

> " From heaven He came and sought her
>   To be His holy bride.
> With His own blood He bought her
>   And for her life He died."

God can get servants anywhere and everywhere,

> " Say not my soul from whence can God relieve thy care,
>   Remember that omnipotence hath servants everywhere."

but God cannot find *sons* everywhere, and the service begotten of the spirit of true sonship is so very precious to God.

Joseph brings us to the *crown all*, viz. rule acceptable to God, the ultimate consequence of the fulfilment, in their growth and development, of the preceeding *types* in our inmost soul. *Elders*, " To the elders which are among you I exhort, who am also an Elder " (1 Pet. v. 1), in contrast to, " Not a novice, lest being lifted up with pride he fall into the condemnation of the devil " (1 Tim. iii. 6) that which characterised the men of faith was, they were strangers and pilgrims in the earth. They looked for a city which had foundations, whose builder and maker is God (verse 10). They lived on the promises, *saw* them afar off, were *persuaded* by them and *embraced* them (verse 13). All these great examples of faith, concerning whom God says the world was not worthy, obtained a good report. Yet! obtained not the promises. Why? God having provided some better thing for us, that they without us should not be made perfect (verse 40). The promises of eternal inheritance made to Abraham, Isaac and Jacob could only be received in resurrection (compare Exod. vi. 4 with Acts vii. 5). In Hebrews xii. 23 we have "the spirits of just men perfected," *i.e.* glorified and perfected in resurrection. They will come in for theirs *when* we come in for the better things provided by God for us. We and they will have the fulfilment in resurrection. "The resurrection of the just" is God's great answer to, and triumph over, sin and death, both in His creation and in His saints, and all the fruit of His cross.

ANALYSIS OF CHAPTER

FAITH'S PORTRAIT GALLERY OF GOD'S GREAT DEAD.

SUBJECT: Faith.

QUALITY OF FAITH (vv. 1-3).

1. The substance of hope.
2. The conviction of the unseen.
3. Begets a good report.
4. Gives spiritual understanding.
5. Interprets Genesis i.
6. Denies evolution.
7. Acknowledges a Divine Creator.

Types of Faith.

I.—Abel (*i.e.* vanity). *Saving Faith.*
  1. Faith at the Cross.
  2. Faith a worshipper.
  3. Constituted righteous.
  4. Obtains God's testimony.
  5. Ever lives.

II.—Enoch (*i.e.* dedicated). "*The Walk of Faith.*"
  1. Walked with God.
  2. Translated by God.
  3. Testimony left ; He pleased God.

III.—Noah (*i.e.* Rest). "*The Testimony of Faith.*"
  1. Faith listening. "Warned of God."
  2. Faith obedient and active. Built an Ark.
  3. Faith testifying. "A preacher of Righteousness" (2 Peter ii. 5).
  4. Faith accepting. "He went in."
  5. Thus condemned the world.
  6. Inherited "the righteousness of Faith."

IV.—Abraham (*i.e.* Fruitful father). "*The Obedience of Faith.*"
  1. Faith risking. "He went out" (v. 8).
  2. Faith in the dark. "Not knowing whither he went" (v. 8).
  3. Faith prospecting. "He sought a country" (v. 14).
  4. Faith in separation (v. 15).
  5. Faith fruitful (v. 11).
  6. Faith surrendering (v. 17).
  7. Faith justified (James ii. 21).
  8. Faith at the Cross. "Offered up Isaac" (v. 17).
  9. Faith at the Tomb. "Received him from the dead."

V.—Isaac (*i.e.* Laughter). "*The Sonship of Faith.*"

Faith's surrender. " Bound " (Gen. xxii).
Faith's sacrifice. " To the Altar."
Faith's vision. " Things to come " (v. 20).

VI.—Jacob (*i.e.* Supplanter). "*The Service of Faith.*"

Faith in blessing (v. 21).
Faith a worshipper.

VII.—Joseph (*i.e.* He will add). "*The Rule of Faith.*"

Faith's vision. Foresaw the Exodus (v. 22).
Faith commanding. " Concerning His bones."

VIII.—Moses (*i.e.* Drawn out). "*The Separation of Faith.*"

1. Faith's confidence (v. 23). " Hid three months."
2. Faith's beauty. A proper child (margin). " Fair to God " (v. 23).
3. Faith's maturity. " Come to years " (v. 24).
4. Faith's refusings (v. 24).
5. Faith's Choice. Affliction with God's people (v. 25).
6. Faith's estimate. The reproach of Christ (v. 26).
7. Faith's respect. The judgment-seat (v. 26).
8. Faith forsaking. The world. Egypt (v. 27).
9. Faith fearless (v. 27).
10. Faith enduring. Seeing the unseen (v. 27).
11. Faith at Calvary. Kept the Passover (v. 28).
12. Faith's deliverance and separation. Red Sea (v. 29).
13. Faith warring. Jericho (v. 30).
14. Faith saving and delivering. Rahab (v. 31).

FAITH'S GREAT HEROES AND THEIR VICTORIES
(v. 32).

1. Gideon,   *i.e.* Feller Down.
2. Barak,   *i.e.* Lightning.
3. Samson,   *i.e.* Sonlike.
4. Jephthae,   *i.e.* He will open.
5. David,   *i.e.* Beloved.
6. Solomon,   *i.e.* Ask of God.

THEIR VICTORIES (vv. 33-35).

1. Subdued Kingdoms.
2. Wrought righteousness.
3. Obtained promises.
4. Conquered lions.
5. Quenched fires.
6. Escaped the sword.
7. In weakness made strong.
8. Valiant in fight.
9. Overcome their oppressors.
10. Raised the dead.
11. Obtained a good report (v. 39).

These victories were in the Land of Canaan, and are typical of our warfare in the Heavenlies (*see* Eph. vi. 12).

FAITH'S SUFFERINGS AND MARTYRDOM (vv. 35-39).

1. Mocked and scourged.
2. Bound and imprisoned.
3. Stoned and slain.
4. Sawn asunder.
5. Wandering and destitute.
6. Afflicted and tormented.
7. Refusing deliverance.
8. Dying triumphant in Faith (v. 39).

Words used in this chapter, and nowhere else in the New Testament :—

1. ελεγος—elegos (v. 1), translated "evidence."

2. ευηρεστηκεναί—euerestēkenai (v. 5), translated "pleased."

3. **Μεταθεσεως**—metatheseōs (v. 5), translated "translation."

4. **Μίσθαποδοτης**—misthapodotēs (v. 6), translated "rewarder."

5. **Δημίσυργος**—demisurgos (v. 10), translated "builder." Revisers margin give "architect."

6. αναρίθμητος—Anarithmētos (v. 12), translated "innumerable."

7. **Δίαταγμα** —diatagma (v. 23), translated "commandment."

8. **απεβλεπεν**—apeblepen (v. 26), translated "had respect."

9. **εκαρτερησεν**—akartēresen (v. 27), translated "endured."

10. **Ολοθρευων**—olothreuōn (v. 28), translated "destroyed."

11. **Προσχυσίν**—proschusin (v. 28), translated "sprinkling."

12. **συγκακουχεισθαί**—sugkakoucheisthai (v. 25) translated "to suffer affliction with."

13. **Πείραν.**—peiran (v. 29), translated "assaying to do," and in verse 36 there translated "trial."

14. **Κατασκοπους**—kataskopous (v. 31), translated "spies."

15. **συναπλετο**—sunapleto (v. 31), translated "perished."

16. **Κατηωνίαντο**—kateonisanto (v. 33), translated " subdued."

17. **ἐπιλείψει**—epileipsiei (v. 32), translated " would fail."

18. **ἐμπαίγμων**—empaigmōn (v. 36), translated " mockings."

19. **ετυμπανισθησαν.**—etumpanisthēsan (v. 35), translated " were tortured." Revisers give " beaten to death " in their margin.

20. **επρίσθησαν**—epristhēsan (v. 37), translated " were sawn asunder."

21. **δερμασὶν** — dermasin (v. 37), translated " skins."

22. **αγείοις**—ageiois (v. 37), translated " goats."

23. **Κακουχουμενοί** — kakouchoumenoi (v. 37), translated " tormented."

24. **μηλωταὶς**—mēlōtais (v. 37), translated " sheep skins."

25. **Προβλεψαμενου,**—problepsamenou (v. 40), translated " having provided."

Words Nos. 1, 2, 3, 5, 6, 7, 8, 9, 10, 13, 14, 15, 17, 18, 20, 21, 22, 23, 24, 25 are found in the Septuagint version.

CHAPTER XII

CHRIST—FAITH'S AUTHOR AND COMPLETER

IN the preceding Chapters we have had the joy of
meditating on the glories of our Lord. We have
seen Him as Son and Heir. " The impress of
God's substance," *i.e.* " of true Deity possessed."
" Creator," " Sustainer," " Redeemer," " Prophet,"
" Priest," and " King, " Serpent Crusher," greater
than prophets, angels, Moses, Joshua and Aaron,
the true Melchisedec, Minister of the Sanctuary,
Surety and Mediator of the better Covenant, the
Great and Eternal Sacrifice, the Way to God!
Here we are asked to add another title, to heap
more glory upon Him, we are asked to consider
Him as Faith's Author and Leader, Completer and
Consummator !

> " Join all the glorious names
> Of wisdom, love and power
> Which angels ever knew,
> Which mortals ever bore,
> They are too mean to speak His worth,
> Too mean to set my Saviour forth."

He is exalted in manhood as the *perfecter of faith*
in this God-dishonouring scene. Faith applied to
Him is the strongest proof of His true humanity.
In Chapter XI. we had God's own witness to the
past heroes of faith, their testings, sufferings,
triumphs and glories, but at their best they were
all imperfect specimens ; but here we have not
only " Jesus," (please note His human name), as

the perfect example of faith, but also as faith's leader and consummator.

This chapter begins with a stadium, in which the believer is viewed as a competitor in a great race. He is encouraged by the great cloud of testimony-bearers of the past, and he is exhorted to lay aside every weight and sin which so easily beset, and to run with endurance the race, looking off unto Jesus. The suggestion in the cloud of testimony-bearers, is not that those great hearts of a past dispensation are in heaven, and looking this way, I am sure they are not, but the thought is rather that these heroes of faith in their life and death bear witness to us of that which, in a past or present dispensation, gives the victory, " *even our faith* " (1 John v. 4).

These past victors had not the light and truth which we possess, yet! they *overcame*, They had, however, the great fact of God. " For he that cometh to God must believe that He is, and that He is a rewarder of them that diligently seek Him (chapter xi. 6). If this great truth only grips our hearts as an actualised truth, in the power of God's Holy Spirit, what matters anything else! I fear we too often hold it as a matter of doctrine only " Let us " (verse 1), (another of these wonderful " Let us's ") *see* Analysis of Chapter IV., lay aside every weight. This word " weight " is only found here in the New Testament. It is weight in the sense of encumbrance, any thing which would impede our progress, any thing which would hold us back. Many things might be quite legitimate in others, but in this race they must be denied, for in this race every ounce tells.

We ourselves know these weights in our lives, those " Terahs " which so load us, and hold us back, so clog the wheels and encumber us in the race. Some idol, desire, love, cherished thing, snug worldly contentment, prosperity and gain in which we rest and glory, the path of least resistance, no self-sacrifice or denial, having a good time here. The pleasures of this world, the deceitfulness of riches, and worldly ease and prosperity, these are all weights that keep us back in this race. Then there is *sin* which doth so easily beset (here there is no article, and speaks of sin characteristically—sin in its root). If you thought of specialising it you might give unbelief the prominent place, and run with endurance the race that is set before us, looking unto Jesus. This race begins at Calvary, and ends where He is at God's right hand. " The looking off " is the look of faith which imparts to us His strength, and would lead us to say, " I am strong for all things in Christ, who is strengthening me " (Phil. iv. 13). In this life and race of faith He is our great pattern, for He is faith's *author* or *leader*, *completer* and *consummator*. As man He began, and completed perfectly in His own life here, faith, and carried it in its eternal consummation to the right hand of God. Those in Chapter XI. were faith's witnesses and imperfect. He is faith's author and finisher. " The Alpha and the Omega " of *faith*.

As we run this race, meeting obstacles on every hand, experiencing the contest and sufferings of faith, we are exhorted to consider Him, " Jesus,"—again His human name. Consider Him in His enduring such contradiction of sinners against Himself. He trod the same path. He met the same foes. He endured. Not only was He tested by man but He was tested by God. " He endured the Cross, despising the shame, and is set down at the right hand of God," the reward of faith (*see*

Rev. iii. 21). "Consider Him, less ye be weary and faint in your minds." This word "consider" is peculiar to this passage. It really means—to carefully estimate one object with regard to another, or, in other words compare His unparalleled sufferings with the little that you have passed through, for you have not yet resisted unto blood striving against sin, and have forgotten that faith's testing are the trainings of a loving Father. It is for chastening we endure (verse 9, R.V.). Unto you it is given in the behalf of Christ, not only to believe on Him, but *also* to suffer for His sake (Phil. i. 29). Again, beloved, think it not strange concerning the fiery trials which are to try you, as though some strange thing happened unto you. But rejoice in as much, as ye are partakers of *Christ's sufferings*, that, when His *glory* shall be revealed, ye may be glad also with exceeding joy (1 Peter iv. 12-13). In verse 9, we have contrasted heavenly and earthly discipline. The Father of Spirits is contrasted with the fathers of men. His mode of discipline with theirs, and the ends are also contrasted, they for their own pleasure, but He for our profit that we might become partakers of His holiness.

> " The mark of rank in Nature
> Is capacity for pain,
> And the anguish of the singer
> Makes the sweetness of the strain."

For the use of the word translated " exercised " in verse 11, *see* Analysis of Chapter V.

Then comes the needed exhortation of verses 12-15, and also the solemn example of the Apostate Esau, who sold his birthright with all it entailed for a morsel of meat (verse 15). It is a very searching word " Lest any man fail of the grace of God." The participle of the verb here speaks of "a continuous state, and not a single act" —(*Westcott*). Beware less you, too, apostatise, for such a course carries with it "its awful consequences."

The chapter closes with a revelation of the glories of this day of grace over that of law, the glories of Christianity over Judaism, Mount Zion over Mount Sinai, everything connected with Mount Sinai, the giving of the law, was intensely real and visible, something which was literally seen and heard and felt, begetting the deepest possible awe and dread, so terrible was the sight that Moses said, "I exceedingly fear and quake." But faith's sons to-day have not come to that, but to something infinitely *more glorious*. They have come to grace and not law, to love and not fear, to the blood of Jesus and not Abel's, to *Jesus*, the mediator, and not *Moses*, to God Himself, who now speaks from Heaven and not from Sinai, to a Father who deals with you as sons. This being so the exhortation is "See that ye refuse not Him that speaketh," etc. Then comes in one of the solemn words, "*Much more* shall not we escape, if we turn away from Him that speaketh from Heaven," all emphasising the awfulness of the sin of *Apostacy*. The voice that to-day speaks in all the tenderness of grace from heaven is the same voice that shook the earth at Sinai, and has *promised to faith* that He will again shake every shakeable thing that is made, that the fixed and unshakable things may remain. But we, receiving a kingdom which cannot be moved, "Let us have grace whereby we may serve God acceptably with reverence and Godly fear," for "our God is a consuming fire" (verse 28).

ANALYSIS OF CHAPTER

CONTENTS.

1. Exhortation (v. 1).
2. Observation (v. 2).
3. Consideration (v. 3).
4. The School of God (vv. 4-11).
5. Lessons Learned (vv. 12-17).
6. Law and Grace Contrasted (vv. 18-24).
7. Final Exhortation (vv. 25-27).

COMPASSED BY A CLOUD OF

1. Testimony Bearer (chap. ii.) *to*
2. Faith's Reality,
3. Faith's Path,
4. Faith's Suffering,
5. Faith's Glory.

LET US

1. Lay aside
2. Every weight (*hindrances*),
3. Besetting sin (*unbelief*).
4. Run with Endurance.
5. Race set before us.

OBSERVATION.

1. Looking off (*away from self*)
2. Unto Jesus (*His human Name*),
3. Faith's Author,
4. Faith's Completer,
5. Faith's Object,
6. Goal and Pattern.

Sin which doth so easily beset, suggests, because of the subject-matter of Chapter XI., the sin of unbelief. Patience, *i.e.* Endurance and Weights, *i.e.* any hindrance which would impede.

H

CONSIDER HIM (*i.e.* BY COMPARISON).

1. For ye have not yet resisted unto blood.
2. Wax not weary.
3. Fainting in soul.

THE FATHER'S CHASTENING (*i.e.* "TRAINING,"
"CORRECTING ").

1. Forget not.
2. Despise not.
3. Faint not.

ENDURE CHASTENING, *it*

1. Proves His love (v. 6 ; Rev. iii. 19).
2. Establishes sonship.
3. Be subject,
4. It is a wise discipline
5. To produce holiness.
6. Be not bastards, but sons.
7. Example of Training (Romans v. 1-5).

"FATHER OF SPIRITS."

1. Be subject to Him
2. Of spirits (*see*)
3. Numbers xvi. 22 ; Job xxxii. 8 ; Isaiah xlii.
   5 ; Zechariah xii. 1.

THE CHASTENED LIFE (*possesses*)

1. The peaceable fruit of righteousness (v. 11).
2. Strengthens the weak (v. 12).
3. Walks consistently (v. 13).
4. Is no stumbling-block.
5. Respects its birthright. ⎫
6. Is not profane.   ⎬ (vv. 16, 17).
7. Lives a sacred life.   ⎭

OLD AND NEW COVENANTS CONTRASTED.

MOUNT SINAI (*Laws*).	MOUNT ZION (*Grace*).
1. Burning with fire.	1. City of the Living God.
2. Blackness.	2. The "Heavenly" Jerusalem.
3. Darkness.	3. The General Assembly of Angels.
4. Tempest.	4. The Church of the First-born.
5. Sound of a Trumpet.	5. Enrolled in Heaven.
6. Voice of God.	6. God the Judge of all.
7. Fear, Death.	7. The spirits of just men perfected.
8. A terrible sight.	8. Jesus, the Mediator.
9. Moses feared and quaked.	9. The *Blood* of sprinkling.

THE PERIL OF APOSTASY (v. 25).

1. See that ye refuse not
2. Him that speaks.
3. No escape.
4. The same voice.
5. That shook earth (v. 18).
6. Yet once more will shake
7. Heaven also, and
8. Every shakeable thing.

EXHORTATION (v. 27).

1. The Kingdom of God
2. Cannot be shaken.
3. Therefore, let us serve
4. Acceptably,
5. With reverence,
6. With Godly fear, for
7. Our God is a Consuming Fire.

Words found in this Chapter, and nowhere else found in the New Testament :—

1. **νεφος**—nephos (v. 1), translated " cloud."

2. **ευπερίστατον**—euperistaton (v. 1), translated " easily beset." Revisers in their margin give "Doth closely cling to us." This word is difficult to translate, for it is not quoted from any other source (*see* Bishop Westcott's Commentary). It is generally interpreted as some sin peculiar to the individual, for which he has a strong affinity. To me the thought is rather " sin " as the root principle of all evil, *sin* in our nature. Spoken of in Romans as the " body of sin " (Rom. vi. 6). Sin which Romans vi. personifies and deals with, of which John writes and says, " If we say we have no sin we deceive ourselves, etc." (1 John i. 8).

3. **ογκον**—ogkon (v. 1), translated "weight." Revisers in margin give " encumbrance."

4. **αφορωντες**—ophorōntes (v. 2), translated " looking." *Lit.* " looking away."

5. **Τελείωτην** — teleiōtēn (v. 2), translated " finisher." Revisers give " perfecter."

6. **αναλογισασθε**—analogisasthe (v. 3), translated " consider."

7. **ανταγωνιζομενοί** — antagōnizomenoi (v. 4), translated " striving."

8. **αντίκατεστητε**—antikatestēte (v. 4), translated " resisted."

9. **εκλελησθε**—eklelēsthe (v. 5), translated " ye have forgotten."

10. **πρωτοτοκία**—prōtotokia (v. 16), translated " birth-right."

11. **μετεπείτα**—metepeita (v. 17), translated " afterward."

12. **γνοφῳ**—gnophō (v. 18), translated "blackness."

13. **Θυελλη**—thuellē (v. 18), translated "tempest."

14. **Φανταζομενον**—phantazomenon (v. 21), translated " sight." Revisers give " appearance."

15. **Φοβερον**—phoberon (v. 21), translated " terrible." This word is also found in chap. x. vv. 27-31.

16. **εντρομας** — entromas (v. 21), translated " quake."

17. **Πανηγυρεί** — panēgurei (v. 23), translated " general assembly."

18. **ευλαβείας** — eulabeias (v. 28), translated "fear." Also found in chaps. xi. 7; v. 3.

19. **ευαρεστως** — euarestōs (v. 28), translated " acceptably." Revisers give " well-pleasing."

20. **Καταναλισκον**—katanaliskon (v. 29), translated " consuming."

Words Nos. 1, 8, 10, 11, 12, 13, 14, 15, 17, 18, 19, 20, are all found in The Septuagint.

CHAPTER XIII

CHRIST—THE ALTAR SACRIFICE, SHEPHERD AND PRIEST

THIS Chapter, which concludes the epistle, is of an exhortory character, a begetting of a spiritual condition in the hearts and lives of the saints in some measure worthy of the great truths and doctrines dealt with in the letter.

It begins with a command to which in these days, we would do well to take heed. "Let brotherly love continue." The word here for love is "agapy," *i.e., Divine* love, an exhortation to love one another with the love of God It is of this love John speaks when he says, " He that loveth his brother abideth in the light, and there is no occasion of stumbling in him " (1 John ii. 10). The brotherhood of the New Testament is a brotherhood of born again ones, the community of the saints. Compare 1 Peter ii. 17 ; 2 Peter ii. 7 ; 1 Peter iii. 8 ; Romans xii. 10 ; 1 Thess. iv. 9 ; 1 Peter i. 22.

Then comes an exhortation to hospitality (v. 3), reminding them of how some *thus* entertained angels unawares. In this blessed work we have the wonderful example of " *Gaius*." In John's third epistle he is praised for his love of the brethren, and also stranger brethren. This letter bears the date of 90 A.D., but as far back as 60 A.D., Paul writes, saying, " Gaius, mine host, and of the whole church " (Romans xvi. 23.) No doubt in these thirty years, he could speak of a very varied experience in his work of host, of many ups and downs, disappointments, joys and sorrows, in this blessed work to which he had addicted himself, but he still continues, for he did it to, and for, the " Lord Christ," having respect to the recompense of reward, remembering his Lord's words, " Inasmuch as ye did it unto one of the least of these my brethren, ye did it unto me " (Matt. xxv. 40).   In keeping with all this we have a call to true sympathy with our brethren who are passing through trials and difficulties reminding us that we ourselves are still in the body, so, therefore, we know not what yet awaits ourselves.   The marriage state in verse 4 is exalted.   It is a rebuke to a system of celibacy, as well as an exhortation to purity.   Covetousness, in verse 5, is condemned, " Let your manner of life be free from the love of money."   The two vices of uncleanness and covetousness are often linked together (*see* 1 Cor. v. 10 ; vi. 9,10 ; Ephes. v. 3 ; Col. iii. 5).   Love of money and money-grabbing among God's people is a vice for which God would put them away from His assembly (*see* 1 Cor. v. 10).   To realise the wonderful promise of verse 5, a promise full of intensified negatives, " I will in no wise fail thee, neither will I in any wise forsake thee," will be to be saved from the *love of money*, and to be content. Indeed, it will lead us to triumphantly boast in our God, and deliver us from the fear of man.

In verse 7 they are called to remember their guides and to imitate their faith.   These godly men were no longer with them, they had passed away, *but* the fragrance of their memory still remained.   Yes ! they had gone, but the one who was the end of their manner of life still abideth, " Jesus Christ, the same yesterday and to-day and for ever," God's eternal and immutable Christ. The word for end, "*ekbasis*," used in verse 7, is only found elsewhere in Luke ix. 31, where it is translated "decease." 2 Peter i. 15, again translated "decease." 1 Cor x. 13, where it is translated "escape." It does not mean, aim or object, but rather their finale, their exodus from this scene. What was it? Jesus Christ, etc. (verse 8). They not only *began* well, but *ended* well. They *overcame* and kept His works to the end. They finished their course, and their finish was in keeping with all their path, Jesus Christ, Himself, Jesus Christ, the same. Surely these leaders left their fragrance behind, something to remember, now that they had gone.

The argument here for endurance is the immutability of the Saviour. "*Thou remainest*." "Thou *art the* same."

The exhortation in verse 9 is in a tense which marks the danger as being actual. This is a much-needed exhortation in these days, when so many of God's children seem to be in a constant state of flux, having very little fixed or stable doctrine. The antidote is to have the heart established with grace and not with meats. The word for meats here, "bromato," is never used for partaking of sacrifices. These Hebrews had no end of distinctions between "clean" and "unclean," what they could eat and what they must avoid, so much so that it became a fine art among them, and led to unprofitableness. Much of it was made up of God-given distinctions, but to these *simple* and *plain* rules for their conduct, they had added an innumerable list of the traditions of the elders. This question of meats gives the opportunity of bringing in the one sacrifice of Christ, that flesh which is true meat and that blood which is true drink, the sublime truth of the altar Christianity possesses in contrast to the one Judaism possesses. " We have an altar whereof they who are serving the tabernacle have no right to eat " (verse 10). This altar no one serving at Jewish altars could partake of. Note, " of which they that *are serving* the tabernacle have no right to eat." It is this present participle of the verb, which helps to fix the date of this epistle, for at that moment in the temple was the Jewish altar with its ritual.

This section, including verses 10-16, strikingly reveals the types and contrasts of the two dispensations.

We have an altar, whereof they have no right to eat, etc. Why have they no right to eat of it ? Because God forbids it, where ? See the law of the sin offering in Leviticus vi. 30, " And no sin offering whereof any of the blood is brought into the tabernacle of the congregation to reconcile withal in the holy place, *shall be eaten* : it shall be burnt in the fire." This is the strongest argument yet used in the epistle, to separate and keep separate from Judaism. To the Hebrew, God says, abide in Judaism and you cannot participate in Christ's sin offering. To participate therein you must come forth to Him without its camp. It is a reproach, and what a reproach ! but it was and is the reproach which was His who suffered without its camp. To a Jew *then*, to a Jew *now*, this reproach was a very real thing. It meant giving every one and every thing up, and going forth to, Him.

" The homeless stranger outside the Camp."

Peter in his first epistle in chapter iv. 14, 16, has something further to say regarding it. There he gives the Godward side of it, as well as the human, and calls them happy who are so privileged to suffer.

Christ is seen in verse 10 not only as the altar, but also the sacrifice. Altar is a metyphone for the one who sustained it :—

> " Thy Cross alone, O Christ,
> Could bear the awful load
> Which none in heaven nor earth
> Could bear, but God."

He suffered without the gate. He became that kind of sin-offering that Judaism is forbidden to eat. He suffered, to separate the people with His own blood. " Let us go forth, therefore, to Him without its camp bearing His reproach." It is to one who liveth to whom they were to come forth. He who in manhood (for notice His human name, " Jesus,") was the altar and sacrifice, is now in resurrection the great priest. Not only the sin sustaining sacrifice, but now the one who is the true Paschal lamb, who is the food and sustenance of His saints. Not only the bread of God that imparts life, but the bread that sustains the life it imparts. Also the great priest over the House of God, through whom we offer our sacrifices of praise continually, which is fruit of lips confessing His name.

" Fruit of lips " (verse 15) is a Hebraism (*see* Isa. lvii. 19; xxvii. 19; Prov. xviii. 20; Hosea xiv. 2). Hosea scripture renders it " bullocks of our lips."

The other sacrifice is the communion, the holy fellowship of " giving." These are the two sacrifices which God specially emphasises as continually offered to and acceptable by Him through our risen Saviour, outside the camp.

In the exhortation to " obey our guides " (verse 17), there comes in a very solemn word for the guides "who watch for your souls as they that must give an account." Do they who assay to take oversight among the flock, the under shepherds, think seriously of this *solemn warning*. If it means anything, it surely means that God will hold them responsible for the souls of the flock. Oversight is not an office, but a work. "True is the saying, If a man desireth overseership, he desireth a beautiful *work*" (1 Tim. iii. 1). If they are shepherds, indeed, their account will be received as profitable or unprofitable to you (*see* 1 Thess. ii. 19-20). The true leaders in God's assemblies are men whom every godly one gladly obeys. It is not a difficult or an irksome task. It is, alas! the false shepherds which cause most of the sorrow. The word rule in verses 7, 17 and 24, is better translated by *guides or leaders*. In Greek writers the word is applied to military commanders, but it must not be thought of in this sense here, for we remember Peter's exhortation to these leaders, "Neither as being lords over God's heritage, *but* being ensamples to the little flock" (1 Peter v. 3). In connection with true shepherd work comes in the wonderful revelation of the great shepherd Himself alive from among the dead, and *that* through the blood of the eternal covenant. Here our hearts are directed to Him not as the Altar, nor yet the sin-sustaining sacrifice, but as the great shepherd of the sheep, but notice it is the shepherd who died. John x. brings before us very clearly His shepherd death. It does not present Him as laying down His life for the *world*, but for the *sheep*, and all the sheep. The same thought is also hidden here in this great verse. He comes before us not simply as a sin offering, but as a *covenant victim*. "Through the blood of the everlasting covenant." A covenant for which He is the surety (chapter vii. 22) and also the mediator (chapter viii. 6). The linking of our perfecting by God unto the doing of His will, with the resurrected shepherd, is most suggestive. No matter how the under-shepherds may fail and become the anti-type of the evil shepherds of Ezekiel xxxiv, the good or beautiful shepherd Himself who laid down His life for the sheep is now alive again as the great shepherd for evermore, the shepherd and bishop of our souls. Let this wonderful truth so fill and ravish our poor hearts that we may love to go to Him, and casting the arms of our faith around Him cry, with our head pillowed on His bosom.

"Jehovah, my shepherd; I shall not want!" for "He will feed His flock like a shepherd; He shall gather the lambs with His arms, and carry them in His bosom, and shall gently lead those that are with young" (Isa. xl. 11).

ANALYSIS OF CHAPTER

CONTENTS of the closing Chapter.

EXHORTATIONS to

1. Brotherly Love.
2. Hospitality.
3. Fellowship in Suffering.
4. Purity.
5. Freedom from the Love of Money (R.V.).
6. Contentment (vv. 1-5).

THE GREAT DYNAMIC.

His Abiding Promise.
Delivering from Fear of Man (vv. 5, 6).

EXHORTATIONS *re* YOUR LEADERS.

1. Remember them (v. 7).
2. Obey them (v. 24).
3. Salute them (v. 24).
4. Follow their Faith (vv. 7, 8).
5. Considering the Issue (vv. 7, 8).
6. Of their Lives (vv. 7, 8).
7. Jesus Christ (vv. 7, 8).
8. Himself Yesterday (vv. 7, 8).
9. Himself To-Day (vv. 7, 8).
10. Himself for Ever (vv. 7, 8).

THEIR SHEPHERDING (v. 17).

1. Watch for your souls.
2. God demands their account.
3. Either with joy
4. Or with sorrow.

EXHORTATION to (v. 9)

1. Steadfastness in doctrine.
2. Establishment in grace.
3. Inwardly in the heart.
4. Not outwardly with *meats*.
5. Which do not profit : for

OUR ALTAR (vv. 10-12).

1. Is Jesus.
2. The Great Sin Offering.
3. Suffered without the camp.
4. For our separation.
5. The food of God's priests.

EXHORTATION (v. 13).

1. Let us therefore
2. Come forth to Him,
3. Outside the camp,
4. Bearing His reproach.

> Primarily here " THE CAMP " is Judaism. Secondly, any camp in Christendom, where the whole Roasted Lamb of God cannot be eaten and obeyed.

STRANGERS AND PILGRIMS (Through His Cross, v. 14).

1. Here we have
2. No continuing city.
3. We seek one
4. That is coming.

EXHORTATION to (v. 15)

1. Priestly worship.
2. To offer up
3. Sacrifices of praise.
4. Fruit of lips.
5. Continually
6. Confessing His Name.

THREE ESSENTIALS to all true Confession is

1. Attachment to His person.
2. Dependence on His work.
3. Devotion to His service.

MANWARD (v. 16).

1. Good works forget not.
2. Communicate, for
3. These sacrifices
4. Please God.

THE GREAT SHEPHERD. HIMSELF (v. 20).

1. The Great Sacrifice.
2. The Great Shepherd of the Sheep.
3. Raised by " the God of Peace "
4. Through the Blood of an
5. Everlasting Covenant,
6. From among dead ones.

THE GOD OF PEACE IN BENEDICTION (v. 21).

1. Make you perfect.
2. In every good work,
3. To do His will.
4. To be well pleasing
5. In His sight.
6. Grace be with you all.—Amen

" PARTAKERS "

1. Of the heavenly calling (chap. iii. 1).
2. Of Christ (chap. iii. 14).
3. Of the Holy Spirit (chap. vi. 4).
4. With the martyrs (chap x. 33, R.V.).
5. Of chastisement (chap. xii. 8).
6. Of His holiness (chap. xii 10).

" ETERNAL " IN HEBREWS.

1. Thy throne . . . is for ever and ever (chap. i. 8).
2. Thou art a Priest for ever (chap. v. 6; vii. 21).
3. Eternal salvation (chap. v. 9).
4. Eternal judgment (chap. vi. 2).
5. Eternal life (chap. vii 16, 25).
6. Perfected for evermore (chap. vii. 28).
7. Eternal redemption (chap. ix. 12).
8. The Eternal Spirit (chapter ix. 14).
9. Eternal inheritance (chap. ix. 15).
10. Eternal sacrifice (chap. x. 12).

11. Perfected for ever (chap. x. 14).
12. Jesus Christ the same for ever (chap. xiii. 8).
13. The everlasting covenant (chap. xiii. 20).

List of words found only in this Chapter, and nowhere else in New Testament :—

1. **κακουχουμενων** — kakouchoumenōn (v. 3),
   translated " suffer adversity." Revisers
   render " evil entreated." This word is also
   used in chap. xi. 37.

2. **συνδεδεμενοί**—sundedemenoi (v. 3), translated
   " bound with."

3. **ευπομας**—eupomas (v. 16), translated "to do
   good."

4. **'Υπείκετε**—hupeikete (v. 17), translated "sub-
   mit."

5. **αλυσίτελες**—alusiteles (v. 17), translated unprofitable."

Words Nos. 1 and 2 are found in The Septuagint.